DARJEELING PIONEERS

Sophie Stölke

Darjeeling Pioneers

The Wernicke - Stölke Story

Fred Pinn

Pagoda Tree Press
2003

Darjeeling Pioneers
The Wernicke Stölke Story

First Published in 2003
By
Hugh Ashley Rayner
at the
Pagoda Tree Press
4 Malvern Buildings, Bath BA1 6JX, Somerset. England.
www.pagodatreepress.com
Email enquiries: *hughrayner@pagodatreepress.com*

© 2003 Fred Pinn.
The moral right of the author has been asserted.

Printed at the Pagoda Tree Press, Bath

A Catalogue record for this book is available from the British Library.

ISBN: 1-904289-01-0
UK Price: £16.00

Contents

Illustrations.

INTRODUCTION

"What made you choose the topic of the Moravians and the Wernickes in particular?" has been an often repeated question. The answer is: "I didn't, they chose me." It really started with a Christmas present of a packet of Darjeeling tea sent with a pamphlet on *"The German Tea Planters At Darjeeling"* and later, a Xeroxed copy of the reminiscences of Sophie Wernicke — *"The Life History of an 85 year old Missionary Widow."* The tea was drunk with much pleasure and the printed matter was turned into a booklet for the entertainment of the German guests at the "Windamere Hotel" in Darjeeling; an English translation was planned for later. That was 1994/95.

In March 1997 I was introduced to a Mr. Etienne Verniquet. My immediate reaction was "That sounds like Wernicke." "It is," was the rejoinder. (More about the name elsewhere.) We met again and Mr. Verniquet showed me several rare Wernicke family photographs and a number of documents compiled by Mr. Timothy Davies, another member of the Wernicke clan, all of which was most generously put at my disposal for scrutiny. I decided there and then that all this material was exciting evidence of the development of early Darjeeling and had to be published. In fact, the German's letters are among the first personal accounts of life at Darjeeling as experienced by resident European inhabitants of the hill station — the pioneers.

From missionary to tea planter — the Wernicke-Stölke story is a tale of great hardship, endurance, determination and great faith, and incredible from the outset: The year is 1838. An English Baptist missionary, William Start, goes from Bristol to Berlin where he had heard the Gossner Mission had people willing to go abroad to preach the Gospel to the "heathen." Pastor Gossner finds several very young men and women from two villages near Berlin who without further ado pack their minimum of luggage, say "goodbye" to their parents and siblings (whom they will never see again!) and follow the Englishman. The understanding is that they will earn their keep by farming whilst at the same time engaging in missionary work. They are blissfully ignorant of India, its climate, languages, culture and — most important — Indian agriculture. Things were bound to go wrong. They were moved from one place to another, illness took its toll; one baby died, food was difficult to obtain; and the "heathen" - mostly Muslims! - were extremely hostile. Mr. Stuart turned out to be a rather autocratic and inconsiderate man who decided all their movements without consultation. At Darjeeling, though they were yet unable to support themselves completely, he withdrew his financial assistance from one day to the next and told them to leave their communal bungalow and fend for themselves. It was swim or sink — they swam .... True, he lent them some money to tide them over but he charged "his missionaries" interest on the loan! However, in spite of the rough sea they swam and landed .....

The first generation of Wernickes and Stölkes took their share in clearing the jungle around Darjeeling, constructing bungalows, producing enough farm products to sell to the summer visitors and running a general store. In whatever time they could spare — which was little enough — they tried to continue their missionary efforts but .... no converts.

The second and third generation of Wernickes and Stölkes were good Christian men and women but devoted themselves entirely to the growing of the precious tea plant. But that is another story .....

There have been hints and sniggers that the Wernickes had left the Gospel for the more remunerative tea, though it is quite clear that they had been forced to minimise their missionary activities in order to keep their own bodies and souls together. It was the next generation that went into tea and built up what has been called "the Wernicke Empire."

This book has several aims. Firstly: it wants to clear up the confusion over the "Moravians" who did not come from Moravia. Secondly: it hopes to clarify why and how the Wernickes went into the tea business and remove all suspicion of greed or similar unworthy motives. Thirdly, it is meant to demonstrate the contribution the Wernickes and Stölkes made to the development of the tea industry of Darjeeling, and fourthly; this compilation of rare sources is given in full text for future students of the history of Darjeeling in view of the inaccessibility of the material used; this is meant to be a source book.

Acknowledgements:

I am greatly obliged to Timothy Davies (the archivist of the Wernicke clan), for the generous loan of his entire collection of family documents and illustrations, without which this book could never have been produced. I am similarly most grateful to Etienne Verniquet, for generously putting at my disposal family photographs, which have proved invaluable as illustrations. I must thank Klaus Simon for instigating this book, when he sent me a copy of the german text of the original work by Paul Gerhard & Sophie Wernicke, The people of Grosswulkow, especially Pfarrer Stephan , for their great hospitality during my research visit there in 1999; James Sinclair, (Great Grandson of William Sinclair and Lizzie Wernicke), for digitising my typescript, and also Hugh Rayner, for his efforts in bringing this book to publication.

Fred Pinn, London May 2003

Publishers Footnote: Fred Pinn passed away on the 19th July 2003, aged 85, just as the final proofs of this book were completed.

THE MORAVIANS AT DARJEELING

The "Moravian" label given to the German missionaries — turned tea-planters — at Darjeeling has caused much confusion in the past. It was mostly assumed that those people had come from Moravia (now Czechoslovakia) whereas, in fact, they had originally been farmers for generations in the Mark Brandenburg close to Berlin. It is, therefore, of some interest to trace the Wernicke-Stölke story to its beginnings.

"The Moravian Church" is a Protestant denomination found in the 18th century but tracing its origin to the *Unitas Fratrum* (Unity of Brethren) of the 15th century Hussite movement in Bohemia and Moravia.

During the 16th and 17th centuries, the Bohemian Brethren movement survived suppression by the Counter-Reformation and proscription by the Peace of Westphalia (1648) through the efforts of a so-called hidden seed of loyal adherents. In the meantime Protestantism in general had lost some of the vitality of its beginning. Revival came in the form of German Pietism in the late 17th century, increasing the unrest among the underground Protestants in nearby Moravia and Bohemia. Flight to Protestant regions of Germany became widespread, and Pietism had a profound influence upon many of the nobility. Thus it was that the young Count Nikolaus Ludwig von Zinzendorf became the agent through whom the "hidden seed" was restored.

A group of families, adhering to the tradition of the Bohemian Brethren, fled Moravia in 1722 and settled on the Count's estate in Saxony, where they founded Herrnhut. The village almost immediately attracted a growing stream of exiles from Bohemia and Moravia, as well as Pietists from Germany and beyond. The community worshipped and partook of the sacraments in the Lutheran parish church of the adjacent village of Berthelsdorf. There were also many extra church services in an assembly hall in Herrnhut.

The Count, a devout Lutheran, tried to keep the refugees within the state church. His aversion to what seemed like sectarianism, was overcome when he realised that he was confronted with a remnant of a church older than his own.

Reluctantly he helped them to revive their own tradition, though the ultimate development was twofold. Herrnhut became the mother community of what came to be called the Moravian Church. It also became the centre for a network of societies on the established Pietist pattern, working for the nurture of spiritual life within the state churches, mostly Lutheran, but also including some Reformed churches. This latter phase of Moravianism on the Continent became to be known as the "diaspora" and its members far outnumbered those who belonged to the Moravian Church as a denomination .....

"*Herrnhut developed a unique type of community in which civic and church life were integrated into a theocratic society, a prototype for about 20 such settlements in Europe, the British Isles, and America. Christian nurture through fellowship groups, daily worship featuring both singing and instrumental music, boarding schools, and concentration on foreign missions and diaspora evangelism characterised these exclusive Moravian villages. They supported themselves and their projects by thriving handicraft industries .....*" (Encyclopaedia Britannica)

From the above account it becomes clear that the small band of German missionaries at Darjeeling had taken Herrnhut as their model, though they had not come under the auspices of the Moravian Church but as members of the Gossner Mission in Berlin. There were, however, close contacts with Herrnhut. Thus Sophie Wernicke, at the age of 85, is described by her interviewer and editor of her autobiography, as "*still wearing the becoming white bonnet of the Herrnhuter, tied with a pink ribbon, to whose community she once belonged.*" Her younger brother, Johannes, too was closely connected at one time, for he was at school at Gnadau, a Herrnhuter settlement, where he received his education. The other missionaries were villagers of the Mark Brandenburg who had come under the powerful influence of the Herrnhuter movement without being members of the "Brotherhood" ("*Brudergemeine*"). But to outsiders the finer differences between the splinter groups were unknown, and Lutheran, Pietist, Herrnhuter, Zinzendorfer and Moravian were all synonymous concepts. And so, the Wernickes, Stölkes and Niebels all became "Moravians", in Darjeeling.

Pfarrer Ferdinand Hachtmann

Three clergymen played an important part in the Wernicke-Stölke story: Pfarrer Hachtmann, Pfarrer Gossner and the Rev. Start. It was Pfarrer Hachtmann who started it all. He had come as a parish priest to Klein and Grosswulkow in 1829 all the way from Silesia, a fact which was interpreted by some parishoners as a sign of God's special concern for their villages. But the "living" was not really satisfactory, for it was said that "he arrived poor and left poorer"; indeed, at one point he had to appeal to the church authorities for funds to buy some clothes for himself and his family. However, though his outward appearance was not impressive, his personality was most powerful and had a great and lasting influence on his parish. Unlike most clergymen of his time, whose sermons were concerned with theological topics which a village congregation would find above their understanding, Hachtmann concentrated on the personal relationship of each villager with God and the daily putting into practice of the Bible's teaching; in short, instead of appealing to the intellect of the individual, he tried to awaken his conscience. His sermons were so rousing that many members of the congregation would follow him from one church to another on days when he had to hold services in different churches, so that he had to preach a new sermon each time. This does not seem to have caused him any difficulty, as he was an inspired preacher who needed no written notes for his messages. Among Hachtmann's many activities was the introduction of an interest in mission work, with the result that several young people in his parish volunteered to go abroad, to America and India, such as the Wernickes of Klein-Wulkow, and the Stölkes of Glöwen.

2. Pfarrer Johannes Gossner

JOHANNES EVANGELISTA GOSSNER

The Gossner Mission is one of the few German missionary societies that bears the name of its founder. It is a sign of the decisive importance which Gossner's thought and faith has had for the history and structure of the Mission and which it retains today.

Johannes Evengelista Gossner was born on the 14th December, 1773, in Hausen near Ulm. In 1796 he entered the priesthood of the Catholic Church. Because of his close relationships with the movement for renewal, tension soon developed between himself and the Catholic Church. Gossner had to endure numerous moves and humiliations which eventually led to his confinement in a penitentiary for priests.

In 1819 the Czar Alexander I of Russia summoned Gossner to the Roman Catholic Maltese Church in St. Petersburg. His congregation consisted of all classes, religious allegiances, beliefs and nationalities within the empire and it grew rapidly under his leadership. But the spirit of Metternich and political and religious reaction were far more powerful than Gossner's ecumenical tolerance. By 1824 the Czar caused him once again to be banished from Russia. Gossner's "vagabond years" now followed, during which he became active as a private chaplain in the ranks of the higher aristocracy. With his conversion to the Evangelical Church in 1826 Gossner still clung to the hope of a permanent position as a pastor. He finally received this in 1829 from the Bohemian Lutheran community in Berlin. This was the start of Gossner's missionary activity, which he maintained until his death on the 30th of March, 1858.

His life work

Far beyond his direct personal sphere of influence Gossner was well-known for his pastoral and missionary authorship. He published writings of spiritual direction among which the "*Herzbüchlein*" (The little Book of the Heart) and the "*Schatzkästchen*" (The little Treasure Chest) are the best known. By his friendship with Boos, Sailer and Spittler, members of the movement for renewal, Gossner became acquainted with a new and nascent missionary surge. At first he devoted himself primarily to the sphere of home mission, and in 1833 founded a Christian nursing community. Soon after he brought into being the first children's nursing homes. Later, in 1837, the Elizabeth Hospital, which still stands today with its own nursing sisterhood, grew out of the original nursing community.

His active participation in wider mission began in 1831, when Gossner was appointed to the committee of the Berlin Missionary Society, which had just been established. However his membership of the Berlin Missionary Society did not last very long, because in his usual logical and insistent way he entertained a fundamentally different conception of mission. In the first place he maintained that a full scientific and theological training was not necessary for those missionaries, who were to be sent to such peoples as were themselves devoid of a similar educational background. Furthermore he refused to countenance the building of mission houses, for he feared that thereby the funds for the mission would be diminished. Moreover he considered that the construction of such property would generate an administrative system which was unnecessary and that the consequential regulations and ordinances would only serve to hinder the free workings of the Spirit of God.

In leaving the Berlin Committee Gossner's missionary work was by no means over. On the contrary it began in earnest. Gossner began to publish his periodical "The Bees in the Missionfield," in which from 1834 he published missionary news from all over the world and by 1837 he was despatching the first twelve missionaries to Australia. Of these, only one was an ordained student of theology, the remainder being craftsmen and farmers.

Gossner had spent half a year preparing them for their missionary role. In an unmistakable similarity to the missions of the Herrnhuter Brethren, those missionaries sent out by Gossner were to be active on the apostolic pattern, that is to say they were to preach the Gospel and in the meanwhile were to be responsible for their own means of livelihood. They received no funding. The Confessional Church was to play no part in Gossner's epiphany. In this way he could place those missionaries, which he himself had trained, at the disposal of any and every missionary society.

In spite of his industrious missionary activity Gossner began by striving against the founding of any kind of missionary society. Only after pressure on the part of the Church and the state was the "Evangelical Missionary Union for the Extension of Christendom among the Natives of Heathen Lands" brought into being in the year 1842. In its statutes, matters to do with dogmatic allegiance, church order and the training and the financial support of missionaries were regulated.

The world-wide Gossner mission.

In Gossner's lifetime altogether 141 missionaries and 60 missionary Sisters and wives were sent out into all the continents. Among them there were only 16 academically educated theologians. Steady missionary work by Gossner missionaries developed particularly in two areas of North India. While the Ganges Mission was transferred to the Anglican Church during the First World War, the mission among the primitive peoples of Chota Nagpur was settled in 1919 under the aegis of the "Gossner Evangelical Lutheran Church."

3. Johann Wernicke

4. Gross Wulkow Church

The Rev. William Start

The story of the Wernicke Family is closely linked with the Rev. William Start, for it was he who came to Berlin and from there took Johann Andreas and Sophie Wernicke via England to India in 1838 and thereby completely changed their lives and, unwittingly, laid the foundations for "the Wernicke Empire" (as it has been called). He certainly played a remarkable role in the missionary activities of that period, and his eventual lack of success was chiefly due to his obsessive ambition to "convert the heathen" of India without realising that his ways and means were quite unrealistic and not at all suited to local conditions. His obsession also made him rather insensitive to the needs and difficulties of "his missionaries," and in dealing with which he displayed an unpleasant streak of ruthlessness. Nevertheless, to the outsider he appeared as generous in his support of mission work *"to whom is accorded the honour of being the earliest labourer in the field"* (of Lepcha education in Darjeeling).

Unfortunately, almost nothing is known of Mr. Start before his arrival in India except that he was a man of independent means. He is said to have come to Patna as a chaplain in the East India Company (in 1831?). His name, however, cannot be traced in the records of the "Ecclesiastical Establishment" of the Company, and it must therefore be assumed that he never took up his appointment. His wife was the niece of William Brodie Gurney, the Treasurer of the Baptist Missionary Society, and he, Start, was baptised and joined the Mission in 1831. His arrival, marriage and baptism must all have coincided, and he never entered the "Ecclesiastical Establishment" in the first place. But although he joined the Baptist Mission, he never seems to have been part of it; he rather worked with it, and had his own ideas as to how this should be done ("Mr. Start's Mission" in the "Indian Missionary Directory and Memorial Volume", 1886).

Fortunately, a fairly full and critical survey of missionary activities written by the Rev. William Buyers and published in 1848 (!) in his *"Recollections of Northern India With Observations etc.,"* gives a clear picture of Start's involvement in the various mission stations and some profound comments on the whole organisation of missionary work. It is a valuable document revealing the errors and shortcomings of missionary practices and is worth quoting in toto (with some misconceptions):

"About the year 1832, the Rev. W. Start, originally a clergyman of the Church of England, having devoted himself and his private fortune to the cause of

God in India, settled at Patna, but not in connexion with any society, either of churchmen or dissenters, having not only borne all his own expenses, but contributed with great liberality to the support of other labourers in the field, and also brought out to India a considerable number of useful men from Germany, most of whom are still his assistants in the missions, which he has formed.

Mr. Start had seceded from the Church of England on conscientious grounds, about the time he came out to India, but as far as I am aware, he has never formally joined any other religious denomination. His sentiments are, however, generally regarded as of the same nature, as those usually professed by what are called the Plymouth Brethren, but whether or not, he is considered a member of that body, I am not aware. But though not professing the sentiments of any one denomination, Mr. Start has generally, with much catholicity of feeling, and Christian liberality, more or less assisted, and held communion with all, both by personal intercourse, and pecuniary contributions. His principal efforts, however, have been directed to the formation of what he hoped would be "self supporting missions," composed of plain Christian men, who, by forming small colonies among the heathen, might be able, both by teaching and example, to recommend the gospel to their attention, while by working at their respective businesses, they might obtain their own temporal support; thus bearing the character, more of witnesses among the people, than that of men exclusively devoted to public teaching. To carry out this plan, Mr. Start has brought at several times from Germany, I think, about twenty young men. A few of these have been ordained ministers, some schoolmasters, but the greater part, mechanics. Besides at Patna, these assistants of Mr. Start, are now settled in several parts of the country, such as Gaya and Arrah, to the south of the Ganges in Bahár, and at Hájipur, Chapra and Muzaffurpur, to the north, besides at Darjeeling on the lower range of the Hamalaya mountains. All these stations, have hitherto been supported by Mr. Start himself, with, perhaps, some aid from a few friends holding similar sentiments. These German missionaries in Mr. Start's connexion, are not generally considered to be under any engagement, either expressed or understood, to remain with him permanently, or to preach his peculiar views. In fact, some of them do not seem to have been aware, when they joined him, that he held sentiments at all different from what are usual among evangelical Churches. This subsequently led to some uneasiness in the minds of several of them, as they seemed to think, that while he did not in the least interfere with their liberty of conscience, he was not a little disappointed to find, that they had not fallen more readily in with his sentiments. While some of them also, were able to go on comfortably in secular business, did not at all comport with their usefulness as missionaries, in a country where studious, as well as active habits, are so much required, as in India.

It is not improbable that the plan might have succeeded better in South Africa, or some other country, whose natives were in a ruder state, and where, from the demands of a colony, greater encouragement might have been given, to men who could support themselves by mechanical labour. But in India, where almost every sort of business, or art, is already practised with more advantage by the natives themselves, there was little room for success in any ordinary trade, unless at the sacrifice of such an amount of time, labour, and close attention to business, as would render all efficient study, and well directed missionary efforts, next to impossible. To say that the plan has been a failure, might be saying too much, but there has, as yet, been little appearance of the hopes of its pious, and benevolent promoter, being realized to any great extent. Some of the German missionaries, who have come to India in this way, have since preferred connecting themselves with different societies. Two are now in connection with the London society, at Benares and Mirzapur, and several others have joined the Church, and Baptist societies. Some of them previously held Baptist sentiments, and, therefore, very naturally inclined to that body, while others, having in Germany been Lutherans, were more disposed towards the church of England. As the whole mission is dependent on Mr. Start, who is now in England, there seems to be little prospect of permanency in its operations, unless something is done to give it more organized support. Were its founder, and almost sole supporter, removed by death, the whole body would be, almost of necessity, dissolved, though its agents might not be lost to India, as most of them would likely be supported, either by individuals, or societies."

Obviously, the Rev. Buyers was well informed on what was going on in the various mission stations. His observations on the impossibility of competition with Indian craftsmen and traders were taken up again in the "Calcutta Review" where a writer remarked with reference to Darjeeling: *"Europeans cannot gain a livelihood as tradesmen in competition with natives,"* and Hathorn in his "Handbook Of Darjeeling" (1863) commented: *"That this is a mistake so far as Darjeeling is concerned, is proved by the fact that the three Germans who left the mission work have without exception gained a livelihood as tradesmen, and one of them at least is now in comfortable if not affluent circumstances. We must look elsewhere for the cause of failure. We are not disposed to enter on the subject at length, or to criticise the acts of so excellent a man as Mr. Start, but we conceive that some of his arrangements, however well intentioned, must have given umbrage to the Germans, and without coming to a positive rupture it was thought better to dissolve the connection, the mission being henceforth carried on conjointly by Mr. Start and Mr. Niebel,"* (who was a Baptist!)

The existence of a Lepcha school at Tukvar is rather puzzling. According to A. R. Foning ("Lepcha My Vanishing Tribe") the Rev. Mr. William Start established a school in 1841 just below the present St. Joseph's College, at Tukvar. Seeing the pitiable and backward condition of the Lepchas, he tried to improve their condition through education. At the same time he tried to convert them to the new faith of Christianity, which he thought would bring an all-round improvement among these unfortunate beings. He employed the Moravian system of education, almost similar to the one advocated later by Mahatma Ghandi in India for his Basic Education. It was the learning of the three "R's," along with the learning of a trade for the student's own upkeep while at school and for learning a trade for the future. Later, he would be able to earn something through his trade and, thereby, he would be able to supplement his insufficient income from agriculture, which was his sole means of livelihood. These missionaries thought that this would improve their economic condition. This school may have been started but soon enough must have fizzled out for lack of pupils, like the other attempt of which Stölke reported in 1854 when local people refused to send their children to a government school, let alone a mission school, for fear of "corruption" or "pollution." This is just another example of the execution of good ideas that went wrong because of Start's unrealistic approach.

Although Tukvar as a school was a non-starter, it served some educational purpose: Between 1841 and 1849 Start seems to have stayed mainly at this estate together with the Rev. Niebel, and engaged entirely, or almost so, in the translation of Biblical texts, sermons and tracts, as were common at the time, into Lepcha. Actually, it is not sure at all where he stayed, as he had at least two more properties at Darjeeling marked on the 1862 map as "Mr. Start's Houses." One can easily imagine him retiring to his other "houses" when he had had enough of the company of those unsatisfactory German peasants who could not learn Hindustani, Lepcha, Nepali and English as fast as he expected and do a day's work in the jungle to earn a living, and ..... Sophie Wernicke has a few stories to tell .....

In 1849 the Committee of the Baptist Missionary Society decided to relinquish the Society's station at Patna, but *"having read a copy of a letter from Mr. Start to Mr. Thomas, dated July 25th, from which they learn his desire and intention to occupy that station ..... the Committee authorize the Calcutta brethren to make such arrangements as to the Society's property at Patna as they think fit."* (Oct. 9, 1849) Mr. Start moved in to the station.

Mr. Start finally returned to England (Bristol?) in 1852 for health reasons, though his intention at the time was to go back to India; however, *"the medical men have positively forbidden it."*

Ten years later, in 1862, Hathorn concluded his eulogy of Start by saying: *"He is now in England, compelled by old age and ill health to relinquish those personal labours in which his earlier years have been passed."*

Thus Hachtmann, Gossner and Start between them talked the young Wernickes and Stölkes into entering on a career of missionaries, an occupation of which these German farmers could only have had the vaguest notion. They cannot have been aware of being uprooted from the soil that had been ploughed by their forefathers for generations, nor can they have had the slightest idea of the implications of living conditions they were going to face in India.

The Wernickes had been farming in Kleinwulkow in the Mark Brandenburg before 1667; in fact, they were a widely spread clan assumedly originating from a village called Wernikow (near Wittstock). The Stölkes were farmers at Glöwen (ca.40 km north of Kleinwulkow on the Genthin-Jerichow road). In spite of the fair distance between the two villages, there appears to have been a close link between the two families which led to the Wernicke siblings, Johann Andreas (23) and Dorothea Sophia (21) Wernicke, marrying the siblings, Joachim (29) and Sophie Elizabeth (19) Stölke.

From Sophie's account one gets the impression that the whole project was rather sprung on the unsuspecting missionary candidates, who were given little time to ponder the consequences affecting their future lives and that of their children. Sophie Elizabeth, for instance, was called from Gnadau to say "Goodbye" to her brother Joachim, and only there and then decided to join the party and get engaged to Johann Andreas Wernicke.

The whole adventure — for this is what it turned out to be — was written down in some detail by a young member of the Gossner Mission, who greatly admired Sophie Wernicke, and had gone to see her and pay his respects when on a visit to Darjeeling. The next chapter refers to the reminiscences of Sophie Wernicke recorded at Darjeeling in 1903. They are, together with her brother's letters, some of the earliest accounts of living conditions at the newly founded "spa."

Chapter 2

SOPHIE WERNICKE'S MEMOIRS

It is with gratitude that we think of Pastor Paul Gerhard who, in his admiration for Sophie Elizabeth Wernicke, had the courage to ask her for her life story and published it in 1904 for the edification of all those who value compassion, loyalty and determination. It is meet therefore that he should introduce the subject of his veneration in his own words:

"At even time it shall be light" ..... I often thought this to myself, when all day long the heavenly surroundings of Darjeeling were shrouded in dense masses of mist, and then again in the evening, when the clouds had broken up, and the glaciers of the Himalayas were lit with gold by the setting sun and looked over to us with a greeting as if from a better world.

"At evening time it shall be light"; I thought this too during my convalescence in Darjeeling when I visited our oldest living lady missionary, whom Father Gossner had once personally sent out, and when I heard from her mouth how much she had to endure "for the sake of our Redeemer's name" and how nevertheless at the end of her narrative she had burst forth with these words: "The Lord has created everything for the best, yea and all things planned for the best; to God be the glory!" So then I thought in my heart how fine it would be if I, the present day youngest of Gossner's emissaries, were able to write down this interesting and edifying life history so that others might also be delighted by it. My request to this end was gladly granted, and now I invite all friends of the Mission to listen with me to the words of this dear and honourable old lady.

Lady missionary Sophie Elizabeth Wernicke, with her only unmarried daughter who looks after her, lives in a modest little house amongst the splendid villas of the spa town of Darjeeling in a beautiful, almost fairytale environment. It is set upon a wooded mountain slope, which climbs up even higher above the houses; below lies a long valley, already deep in the evening dusk, and looking out towards the distant snow-capped summits of the Himalayas. It is a fitting setting to the story of the lady who lives here. For her journeyings in the deep dark valley lie in the past. She has almost reached the summit of her life story, indeed from the distance they are even now greeting her, "the hills from which cometh our help." But it is a cool October evening — even the year is reaching its end — so we prefer to step from the veranda into the interior of a cheerful living room from which the warming flames of a fire on a open hearth, built after the English manner, flicker invitingly towards us. Close to it sits our gracious story-teller on a low old-fashioned high-backed chair. She still wears the becoming white bonnet, drawn together with a pink ribbon, of the "Herrnhuter" community, to which she once belonged. Her friendly visage is riven by many wrinkles, which the toils and troubles of a life of 85 years have engraved upon it. But the upright bearing of her tall figure, the seraphic words of her speech and the radiance of her eyes testify before us that "at evening time it shall be light."

"It was on the 7th of August 1818 that I was born in the house of my parents in Glöwen near Havelberg in the district of West Priegnitz," lady missionary Wernicke began to tell me, as the grey household cat pressed itself cosily purring against my feet. The following narrative is pieced together from a few short notes in English, which Miss Wernicke has written down, and from the words of Mrs Wernicke, who, although she still speaks clear German, every now and then falls back into the colloquialisms of her present everyday speech, namely English.

"My father, Joachim Stölke, was a wealthy farmer but also an earnest Christian, who brought us children up very strictly. For example we were not allowed to play on Sundays. He would often be encountered singing loudly or praying in the fields or on a byway, but to passers-by he would merely doff his beaverskin cap without allowing any other interruption to his worship. My mother, Elizabeth (née) Herm, was a noble, gentle lady with whom we often sought refuge from the stern ways of our father. Then she would say to us: "Children, do not be unhappy, Father is better than all of us!" There were ten of us in the family, five boys and five girls and we all had to help with the work on our large farm, our brothers in the fields and farmyard, and we girls in the kitchen and spinning-room. When I was 14 years old, I myself went to the Herrnhuter community in Gnadau at the wish of my parents. I had already been living for six years there when, in the middle of June 1838, a letter from my brother in Gross Wulkow arrived, which invited me to join him immediately, for he had received the charge to make his way to Berlin in order to be sent as a missionary in India."

"This was because at the beginning of the year 1838 an English missionary by the name of William Start had come to Berlin to visit Father Gossner with a request for missionaries for his mission in India. At one time Start had been an Anglican clergyman but had then become a Baptist, and, because he was very wealthy, had begun missionary activities on his own initiative in India in 1832 with other missionaries, namely with Messrs Brice, an Englishman, and Kelber, a German. Although Start had had to struggle with many difficulties at the

beginning, including the loss of his wife, he nevertheless returned to Germany at his own expense after a year or two in order to recruit new missionaries for the purposes of the Lord. For this reason he approached Gossner, for he had heard of the great and joyous faith of this man, and also knew that he was preparing missionaries, in order that they might be ready to go forth into any country of the world.

Moreover Father Gossner was in contact with Pastor Hachtmann of Grosswulkow, who was likewise preparing young people for the spreading of the word of God amongst the heathen and at that very time they included Johann Andreas Wernicke, my brother Joachim Stölke and Andreas Dannenberg.

The moment Start had explained his request to Gossner the latter wrote these laconic words to Hachtmann: "Send your young men to Berlin at once, they are urgently needed here." Hachtmann told his young pupils of Gossner's wish. They were only too ready to follow Gossner's famous footsteps and set about preparations for leaving their homeland.

So with my younger brother Johannes, who was at school in Gnadau, I set off for Wulkow to say goodbye to Joachim. When we arrived at Wulkow, Wernicke, whom I had already known from earlier times, very soon came up to me and posed me an unexpected question: would I like to be his companion for life in order to follow him later as a missionary to India. Although with some hesitation, I gladly gave my assent, which was to bring me so much anguish, but also much blessing and joy. The three young men then went off immediately to Berlin, while I and my dear parents, who in the meanwhile had also arrived in Wulkow, returned to Glöwen.

After a few days my father now received a letter from my fiancé, in which he begged him to allow me to leave at once with him for India, as there were now only two married missionaries among the Brethren, and Gossner wished for more. So then I went with all my relations to Berlin, where we soon found our way to Gossner's house, for on the following day the commissioning of the Brethren was about to take place.

The first question that Gossner directed to my father was; "Have you brought your daughter with you from Gnadau?" My father said "Yes!" The next morning it was Sunday and we were called in to Gossner, and there in his room as well as my dear father we found Pastor Hachtmann. Father Gossner's face had a very friendly and winning expression. He was a figure of medium height and extraordinary vigour. As with old Professor Tholuck, one had always to be prepared for unexpected questions in his presence. At the table he was particularly fond of jesting, and with young people he had a habit of personally serving each his portion. One day as he was carving the meat a piece fell by mistake on the ground, whereupon Father Gossner called out to one of the young persons: "Dear son, put your foot on it quickly, so that the dog doesn't eat it!" Thus addressed, the young man immediately complied with the request, but when after a while he removed his foot and examined the piece of meat, he was not a little surprised that in spite of all his precautions, he was now obliged to allow the dog to approach its rightful prey. (Gossner was living together with his 'Cousin Idda', who had earlier been a nun. Since 1803 she had been in charge of the household economy and was called 'Little Aunty' by the other residents).

So when I stepped into Gossner's room on that Sunday morning he asked me if I was ready to become Wernicke's wife, and after I had answered his question with "Yes," he said to me, "Yes, and if Wernicke were to die you would at least have your brother; and if Joachim were to die, then there is still Dannenberg; but if Dannenberg were also called to his rest what then?" I answered "Then there is still the Living God!" At which Gossner said: "It is enough, I see that you are permitted to go forth." I went outside and there was bright sunshine.

But later in the evening after worship we, my fiancé and I, were called in once again to Gossner. He asked us once again whether we were willing to marry and to travel together to India straightaway. We both answered: "Yes." Then Gossner turned to my father, who was finding it very difficult to give up two of his children at the same time, and said: "The Lord said - Let my people go! What have you to say?". My dear father replied: "To that I have no further answer!" That was

5. The Manchester to Liverpool Train

on 1st July 1838.

The next morning the whole missionary company set out upon their long journey, equipped as best she might, by 'Little Aunty,' that is to say she kindly provided - in the greatest haste - the necessary things for myself. The names of the Brethren were as follows; Mr. and Mrs. Brandin, Mr. and Mrs. Treutler, my husband-to-be Wernicke and myself, Messrs Stolzenberg, Stülpnagel, Maas, Joachim Stölke, my brother, Dannenberg, Heining, Nebsch, Baumann and Papproth. These Gossner delivered over to Start with the memorable words: "Continually baptise them daily with the Spirit and with Grace but not again with water!" The next year the same ship brought out more Brethren: Kluge, Schorisch, Sternberg, Rudolf and Ullmann; but these are since all dead.

So, first of all we went by postchaise to Hamburg, a journey which used to last some days. We then transferred by ship across to Hull, where we remained for about a fortnight, and where I was married to my bridegroom, first by a German and then by an English clergyman. On the next day we made use of the very first English railway from Manchester to Liverpool, which everyone regarded as the greatest wonder in the world, but which most people only mounted with the greatest hesitation. At an inn in Liverpool our lunch was already waiting for us. Unfortunately we were only permitted to observe it from afar, for we were immediately summoned to the harbour, because our sailing ship was on the point of setting sail."

The Voyage

In the days of the sailing ships, a voyage from England along the west coast of Africa, around the Cape of Good Hope and across the Indian Ocean to Madras and Calcutta, was an unforgettable experience for any traveller not normally using this mode of transport. A wealthy passenger would have a cabin to himself and even furnish it to his taste and needs, to create the atmosphere of "home from home," for the voyage could take anything from three to six, and in rare cases, nine months and would be very tedious. Sophie is discreetly silent about life on board her ship. Their accommodation could hardly have been more primitive: the "simple boarded partitions between the packing cases" were typical of Reverend Start's belief in training his assistants in "roughing it." It can be assumed that he himself was more comfortable in a cabin of his own. What life must have been like in "the partitions" during the bad weather is left to the imagination of the reader. The indomitable Sophie, still remembering her empty stomach at Liverpool but just hinting at the almost offensive arrangements for their shelter for five long months, continues the account of her crossing the oceans:

"During the next five months we entrusted ourselves to the 'Blorange.' This was the name of our swimming residence, for in those days there was not as yet any Suez Canal but one had to circumnavigate the whole of Africa. Our sailing ship was a simple commercial vessel. It cannot of course be compared to modern rapid ocean-going steamers that are like floating hotels. However, between all the packing cases and sacks of the cargo there had been constructed for each of us, two by two, a simple boarded partition, where we were lodged for the night. There were no other passengers besides ourselves on board. When we stepped aboard there was a high sea running, and as we had eaten practically nothing the whole day, at once we all naturally felt sick and miserable. However after we had overcome this well known sea-sickness, Start called us on deck to teach us Hindustani with the help of a *munshee* (Islamic for Teacher) and for this we used books with the Latin alphabet. We also gathered together morning and evening for community worship and on Sundays we had our normal service, during which the roar of the waves of the ocean seemed to play the part of the organ and repeatedly kept reminding us: *'Oh that thou wouldest hearken to my commandments! Then would thy peace be as a river and thy righteousness as the waves of the sea.'* Now we could enjoy the whole splendour and sublimity of the sea, for after a few days it became completely calm and in the most beautiful weather our sailing ship glided over the endless ocean like a white swan with outspread wings. Round the Cape of Good Hope however a stormy hurricane arose, which wrapped us for 7 days in darkness, so that we could say with St. Paul's travelling companions: *'And when neither sun nor stars shone upon us for many days, and no small tempest lay on us, all hope that we should be saved was taken away.'* As we were sitting at table one day, there was suddenly a tremendous crash so that we were all terribly startled; for everyone thought that we had struck a rock. The ship's officers rushed on deck and after some moments of anxious waiting we were told that the mainmast had broken, but fortunately no one had been hurt in the collapse. Yet *'When need is greatest, God's help is closest.'* Soon after, the storm abated and then we had a peaceful voyage to Calcutta. As we sailed onwards we were met by one more ship, a Chinese one, which had been battered by the storm, and they asked us for drinking water. The request was granted although we ourselves only had very bad supplies, water that was really foul smelling, so that everyone longed to reach the land."

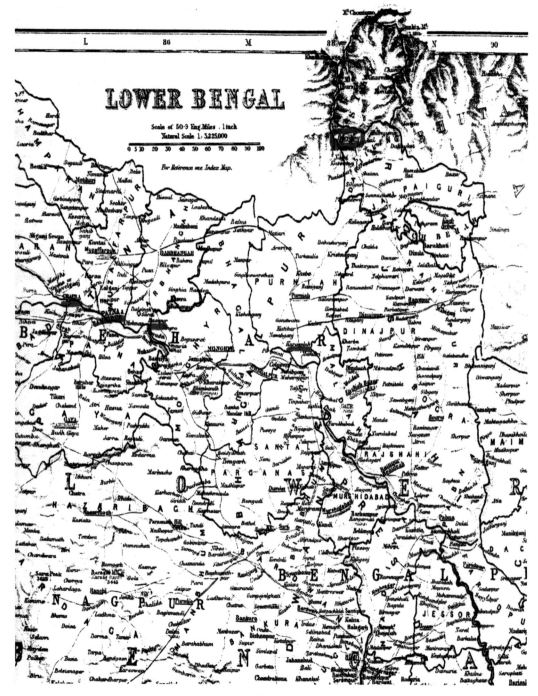

6. Map of Lower Bengal

Arrival in Calcutta

"At the beginning of December we fortunately entered the port of Calcutta and were soon surrounded by a crowd of small boats, in which half-naked natives were offering their wares, particularly fruit. These were the first native people that we had set eyes on, and we ladies were so very much embarrassed by their scanty apparel that we made our way hastily back to our cabins.

7. Calcutta

In Calcutta we were taken in by a missionary family. We stayed with them for about a week in order to make all preparations for the journey up the Ganges to Patna, where Start had set up his own station."

To Patna and Hazipore

It was in January 1839. The "Berliners" were blissfully unaware of all the difficulties the Rev. Buyers knew they would have to face, and so they set out happily on the next leg of their adventurous trip by the common and most comfortable means of transport — the *budgerow*, a popular type of boat which took travellers up and down the Ganges for any stretch or length of time. Mishaps, such as getting stuck on a sandbank, were by far preferable to the discomforts of travelling by road, even though the waterway was longer. It was also the cold weather season and a good time to move about India. Sophie remembered:

8. Travelling Cookboat

"We travelled up the Ganges in three boats: one was for the married members, one for the bachelors, and one was designated the kitchen. At mealtimes the three vessels were manoeuvred side by side and there we ate communally. We also spent the nights in the boats and slept on the plain boards

wrapped in covers. After a voyage of thirty days we arrived at Patna and rested there for a while, but in the evening had to return once again to our boats and after this short break move on towards Hazipore."

Hazipore (Ghazipur)

On Hazipore the Rev. Buyers recorded:

"*There has not been much done to spread the gospel in Ghazipur, and its vicinity. A mission has, however, been formed within the last few years, by the German missionaries of the Berlin society, several of whom have settled here. They are all young men, and are likely to be laborious and useful; but their mission is of too recent origin to be, as yet, expected to have accomplished much. One of the Baptist missionaries, connected with Serampur, settled for a short time here, a number of years ago, but not meeting with encouragement, did not remain long. Sometimes, visits have been paid, and the gospel has been preached, by the church missionaries from Benares, and Chunar, and occasionally by others, but nothing like steady, or systematic efforts, has been made fully to introduce Christianity to the people of Ghazipur, till these German brethren commenced their operations.*

They did not find a very favourable disposition towards the gospel among many of the people; and the Muhammadans, especially, who are numerous, raised rather a strong opposition. It is not at all improbable that the desultoriness of the visits of others, and the want of steady and determined perseverance in the previous attempts made to introduce the gospel, may have given a confidence to opponents, as in some other places of the same kind, which otherwise they would not have had. The European soldiers, also, as in similar military stations, have occasioned no small prejudice against Christianity, by their vicious conduct in the town and neighbourhood, so that a respectful attention to the gospel, has not been

9. Preaching

so easily obtained, as in many other places more favourably situated in this respect. The farther we are from men who call themselves Christians but are not, the easier it is to preach the gospel."

After this background description of *"rather strong opposition"* from the local people with all the attendant obstacles usually encountered in such circumstances, Sophie's tale of misery will not come as a surprise: She says:

"Here (at Hazipore) Start had purchased a large house, which had earlier belonged to the Raja of Nepal. It stood by the river upon a raised platform, from which we could enjoy an enchanting prospect. So here we settled in, by and large without trouble. The only thing was that it was extraordinarily difficult to procure the necessary provisions, although a fine garden belonged to our property. Here, unfortunately, only large tamarind trees grew. So the missionaries began their work here, but as they had not made sufficient progress in the language, they read out to the heathen from tracts. For this purpose they went to the bazaar every morning. About 8 o'clock they returned; we partook of our breakfast and then all windows and doors were closed because of the great heat, and everybody set about studying the language."

The house Start had taken over was the only one maintained in European style; it had been built thirty years earlier by the English because of the dances that used to be held there. The ballroom was transformed into a dormitory and the other twelve rooms were put at the disposal of the Brethren. The women managed the kitchen and the men took up handicrafts. For example, Stölke took instructions from a Mohammedan baker in baking bread and Wernicke took care of the sheep and goats, which he sheared and slaughtered. A year later reinforcements arrived in the shape of Bro. Niebel and five Sisters, some of them wives following their husbands.

At first, manual labour was kept to a minimum, as much time had to be given to the study of the local language; but servants had to be supervised and also observed, in order to learn from them how things were done in India. However, when the budget was suddenly and drastically cut, almost the entire workload fell upon the missionaries. It came as a shock, whose vibrations can still be felt in Sophie's recollection sixty years later:

"After we had settled in with some difficulty, one day a letter arrived from Start, which stirred us all into a great commotion. He demanded that for some 14 people we should only retain three servants, a cook, a watchman and a man from that caste, which undertakes the most servile functions. All other tasks, such as those of butchers, masons, carpenters, gardeners, cobblers, tailors, and all

housework was to be taken over by one or other of the Brethren or Sisters respectively. This would not have meant anything more in a cool climate, but in the hot, low-lying plains of Bengal under the conventions of Indian society this was an absolutely impossible demand. We would have been looked upon as coolies, and all our missionary activities would have been looked upon as pointless, quite apart from the fact that there would have been hardly any time left over for their practice. However, because the necessary cash resources were lacking, we were anyway driven to physical employment and the consequence was that, one after another, we all fell seriously ill with fever and dysentery. To start with I took over the nursing, as I had remained in good health, but later I had to take to my bed through overexertion. Then my husband and I arranged for us to go to Patna, where after a few weeks treatment by the resident doctor we recovered, thank God, and returned to Hazipore. It soon became increasingly apparent here that to carry out the plan of communal work presented considerable difficulty. With Gossner's agreement many of the Brethren therefore transferred to other Missions; two became Baptists and several also died. My husband and I went to Bankipore, where my eldest son Johannes Andreas was born. From Bankipore I had to return in great weakness to Patna, and here the Lord took away from us that which He had just given; our little son died while my husband was on the journey from Bankipore to Patna. This was a hard blow in hard times."

Chupra

Chupra too had not escaped Rev. Buyer's attention:

"A little below the junction of the Dewá with the Ganges, and on the northern bank, is situated the town of Chupra, which is the European station for the neighbouring district. A mission in connection with the Berlin missionary society, has been commenced at this place, as well as one by the Germans, associated with Mr. Start. Their missions are of too recent origin, to have given any reasonable expectations of much actual success as yet, though they have not been without some degree of encouragement. The whole district is one of great importance, and presents a large and interesting field of missionary labour. Chupra itself is not a very compact town, but seems to be formed of a number of separate villages and bazárs. Straggling along the bank of the river, Chupra contains a considerable number of European families. None of the towns in the district are very large, but the country is exceedingly productive, and is covered

with villages, containing an immense rural population. Here the Ganges has shifted its course, so that the town, which once stood on the main stream, is now on a mere branch of the river, which is not navigable in the dry season. Close by the mouth of the Dewá, there is the town of Revelgunj, a place of considerable trade."

Chupra — the last station before the final transfer to Darjeeling, seems to have been a happier place than Hazipore, as Sophie remembers:

"In November Brethren Ullmann and Stülpnagel, my husband and I were sent to Chupra, where we had to live in a very small, uncomfortable house. Later Start bought a government school with a teacher's house, and here we could celebrate worship and some of us lived. Here God sent me my second son, whom I again called Joachim Andreas, and in spite of all the confined living accommodation and many troubles and worries, without which life as a missionary is just not to be contemplated, we all felt very fortunate.

A tale of adventure now comes to mind, which might have had a very serious outcome. One night my husband was quite unable to sleep, and when I asked him why he was so restless, he only replied that he had a feeling that something or other was not quite in order in our house. All my efforts to pacify him were of no avail. Once again my husband got up, walked around the room, listened for a little while and then lay down again to rest. Suddenly he got up again and said to me: 'You there, wife, do you hear nothing? I think there is a body lying under your bed.' At that moment the obvious sound of snoring reached my ears. I leaped up horrified and called out to my brother sleeping in the adjacent room: 'Help, thieves here, help!' My brother came in at once. We looked under the bed, and sure enough there lay a sleeping black figure. My husband and brother Joachim pulled the wretch out by his legs and strong-arm measures made it clear to him that a place under my bed was no sort of sleeping accommodation for him. Then we called the night watchman who was to take this impudent intruder to the police station. The miscreant thus rudely awakened, now adopted energetic counter-measures, protesting that one of us had assaulted him and that he was an Indian Holy Man. In reality he belonged to a band of robbers, who had wanted to attack and rob us that night. The "Holy Man" had crept into the house, so that at a given pre-arranged signal, he could open up from inside. But first of all he had wished to stiffen his nerve with a dose of "Dutch courage" and in doing so the rascal had over-indulged, had fallen asleep and so by his loud snoring had become a traitor to his own disgraceful plot."

BENGAL HURKARU AND INDIA GAZETTEER

Thursday, May 6, 1841

MOFUSSIL: - Darjeeling in April. The very cold, stormy and rainy weather of March, has this month given place to a dry and temperate atmosphere, and builders, road-makers and gardeners have been profitably busy. The pale and sickly looking denizens of the ditch have come thickly to seek refuge and health from their own hot and malarious climate, and the hotel keepers at Titalya, Kurseong and Darjeeling have at length been enabled to commence entries in the credit side of their account books. The arrivals during the month have been more numerous than in March, and as the list of departures is blank, the society is numerous and disposed to gaiety.

Arrivals:- ... The Rev. Mr. Start, Patna ..... Mr. Low ..... Mr. Smith ..
(24 in toto). Mr. Low was the hard-working and most efficient secretary of the "Darjeeling Association" of Calcutta, and Mr. Smith his collaborator and most vociferous promoter of the hill station in his own newspaper the very same BENGAL HURKARU AND GAZETTE.

Darjeeling, 30 April 1841.

10. Lepcha Sepoys

THE BENGAL HURKARU AND INDIA GAZETTEER

November 8, 1841
MOFUSSIL:

MISSION AT DARJEELING — We understand, that three artisan Missionaries of the German Mission at Patna, connected with Mr. Start, are about to be located at Darjeeling. Mr. Start has purchased land there, for that purpose, and has also erected, or is now erecting, a Mission house at the station for himself and friends, and also Mission houses for the permanent Missionary residents at the Bright Spot. The German Mission is conducted on principles very similar to those of the Moravians; they are designed to be self-supporting Missions, and hence the brethren about to (be) located at Darjeeling will not only instruct the heathen in the truths of Christianity, but also in those different branches of labour which may be brought to bear on their present happiness in the increased enjoyment of the comforts of life. Our Brethren have our warmest prayers for their success. **CALCUTTA CHRISTIAN ADVOCATE, November 6, 1841.**

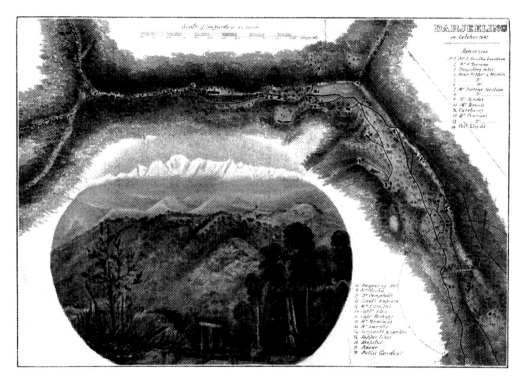

11. Map of Darjeeling in 1841

DARJEELING BEFORE 1842.

According to Hamilton's "EAST INDIA GAZETTEER" the chief who governed Sikkim prior to 1782 by the natives of Bengal was named Roop Chiring whose residence was at Darjeeling where he had "a strong house built of brick and much admired in that region". After the Nepali conquest in 1788 Darjeeling still "appears to have been one of the most important strongholds as it was selected by the Gorkhas for their principal military station."

After the treaty of Segowly in 1817, Darjeeling became the administrative and religious centre for the whole region under a Lepcha chief. The place grew into an important market town and all went well until the (Tibetan) Raja quarrelled with his Lepcha dewan and the entire Lepcha population of Darjeeling fearing the Raja's persecution, abandoned the town in 1827 and fled across the border into Nepal. Two years later the jungle had taken over, and only the ruins of of the brick house and parts of the monastery could be seen when James Grant, the Commercial Resident at Malda, took Col. Lloyd to inspect the site in 1829.

Grant had been at Malda since 1822 and had known Darjeeling from his exploration of the Himalaayan foothills when it was still a lively place and its situation had always impressed him as a suitable hill station. Now the town had been abandoned, Grant tried to impress the Governor-General, Lord William Bentinck, that it would be a most desirable site for a "sanatarium" for the Company's troops, and the kind of hill station the citizens of Calcutta have been clamouring for in imitation of Simla and Ootacamund.

In 1830, Capt. Herbert, the Deputy Surveyor General, visited Darjeeling, also with Grant's guidance, for a "second opinion", which was most enthusiastic and induced the Government to negotiate with the Raja of Sikim for the site.

The rather convoluted negotiations led the Raja finally, for reasons of his own, to make an unconditional present of Darjeeling to the Company in February 1835.

The Government, however, moved very cautiously to avoid mistakes and sent two "guinea pigs" - Col. Lloyd and Dr. Chapman - to spend a year at the future sanatorium to keep records of the weather and their own conditions of health (1836-37). The end result was that Dr. Chapman caused a furious response from all prospective builders of bungalows at the new hill station by declaring Darjeeling as unsuitable, while Col. Lloyd stood by his favourable opinion.

1838 saw the formation of the "DARJEELING ASSOCIATION" which gave the Government any necessary support and did the equally necessary pushing when required.

The following year saw many changes: Col. Lloyd was returned to his army unit without further explanation (on account of mis-management of funds inter al.) and Dr. Campbell took his place for the next 26 years. Lt. Robert Napier came to build the road to the hill station and thereby made his name as a highly successful engineer; and many coolies were brought to Darjeeling, for whom a bazaar was set up.

The newspapers did their bit of positive reporting on every sign of progress. Thus the ASIATIC JOURNAL informs: *"From the intelligence from Darjeeling there was every hope that this delightful sanatarium will be ready for the reception of visitors before the beginning of the next hot season. Upwards of 1200 loads of rice had been sent to it by native merchants. A hundred coolies, with a party of Lepchas, had been employed since the tenth of December (1839) in constructing sheds along the whole line of road for native travellers. Artificers of every description had been engaged at Patna, Rungpore, Berhampore, and Calcutta, and a thousand Dangars (horned cattle) were expected to reach it by the 5th November (1839)";* **Asiatic Journal, April 1840**. And again in May: *"The hotel at Darjeeling was opened on the 31st March, when a party of twelve sat down to dinner. Two good fires kept the temperature at 65 degrees. The place is thriving and facilities for travelling are increasing".*

The BENGAL HURKARU is as busy as ever giving details of Darjeeling in November 1840: *"The only public building is the Superintendant's Cutchery on the Dorjeeling Hill, a neat wattle and dab bungalow with an iron roof. There is an allotment for a church and spaces for public purposes but no appearance of appropriating them. A small fort or neat stockade on the crest of Dorjeeling Hill, where there yet appears the remains of an old monastery, would be ornamental and useful. A good clock is much wanted to regulate the time of the station ... If Government cannot afford a good clock, a good sundial would be very acceptable, and a morning and evening gun would be useful."* Someone evidently approved of the proposal for a sundial, for in 1863, one stood in front of the old Cutchery, *"presented to the station by a visitor"*, possibly as a joke (suggests the author of the handbook of 1863), for, as he says, *"of what use can a sundial be in a place which is always in the clouds."*

Government not only encouraged the use of the new hill station, but set an example by letting it be known to the local papers that *"Mr. Turton, the Advocate-General, proceeds to Darjeeling this day - Thursday, May 7th, 1840 - for the purpose of spending a month in the cooler atmosphere of the mountains. That this may prove as slight an interuption to business as possible, Mr. Turton has, we hear, laid a special dawk for the receipt and transmission of his papers by express. One hundred coolies have been entertained for this purpose and it is computed that the transit from Darjeeling to Calcutta and vice versa will occupy four days and a half."*

A perusal of the *"Bye laws and Office Rules"* at Darjeeling devised by the Superintendant Dr. Campbell in 1841, gives some idea of how life was organised at the hill station:

1. BUILDING sites, of 200 yards square, are granted on a lease of ninety nine years at a rent of Rupees 50 per annum. No more than four sites to be granted to one person, (sanctioned by Government).

2. MESSRS. Hepper, Martin & Co. are making skeleton surveys of the building sites to be lodged in the superintendant's Office. Each settler to pay to the Superintendant Rupees 10 on this account. Copies furnished by the surveyors to the proprietors at 5 Rupees each, complete surveys at Rupees 100 per location.

3. Where clearance of underwood has been made by Government on building ground not assigned, the assignee to pay a clearance fee not exceeding Rupees 50.

4. When the opening of a new road has been decided on, whether at the expense of Government or by the voluntary contributions of settlers, the laying down of such roads to be left to the Superintendant under the advise of the Executive Engineer, and the amount claimable from each subscriber to be regulated by the estimate of Captain Napier. In no case will a station line of road be allowed to interfere with the site of a settler's house.

5. When the objectors to contribute to the making of a road do not exceed one or two of the proprietors on the proposed line, the recusants to be taxed their quota as provided for in Rule 11.

6. When an unfinished public road or proposed line of road forms a boundary to an estate, the proprietor will not put up his railings without a reference to the Superintendant or the Executive Engineer. Along completed roads, railings are not to be put up nearer than four feet below the outer edge or six feet from the upper edge of the road.

7. The amount of "quit rent" and rent to be applied to the making and keeping in repair of station roads and the road from Punkabari to Darjeeling.

8. Each traveller passing a night in the Dâk Bungalows at Siliguri, Punkabari, Mahaldirum and Pucheem, to pay 1 rupee for the use of the same. Travellers halting at the bungalows, merely to take refreshments, to pay 8 annas. The receipt being applicable to their repairs.

9. The rate of 1 rupee per mile, for a set of eight bearers, has been sanctioned on the road to and from Udilpore and Darjeeling, and 8 rupees for a Government elephant from Siligori to Punkabari, and the same from Titalya to Siligori.

The rates at the Siligori Ferry are as follows:

Carriage and pair, . . . 2 0 0	Saddle Horse, ...0 8 0
Buggy, ...1 0 0	Palkee, ...1 0 0

11. One rupee per mensem has been fixed as the rent for a shop in the Darjeeling Bazar for 1841.

12. Prices in the bazar and rates of servants' wages, are left to regulate themselves by the amount of demand and supply, unfettered by Nirikhs or other authoritative interference.

13. A set of standard scales and weights are kept at the Kutchery and in the bazar, for reference in all case of dispute about weight.

14. Drafts on the Treasury, when due, are cashed on all days of the week, Sunday excepted. Stamps are sold on Tuesdays and Thursdays. Civil cases heard on Tuesdays and Fridays. Criminal ones and Police matters on all days at all hours.

15. The dâk leaves Darjeeling at day-light every morning. Letters and parcels "post paid" for dispatch are received at the Post Office from 3 p.m. to half past six p.m. There is a locked box for the deposit of "bearing" and "service" letters at all hours of the day. Letters are distributed immediately after the opening of the daks up to 9 p.m., and after 6 a. m. Bills for postages are not allowed, and travellers requiring bearers are called upon to pay in advance.

16. The bazar sircar is allowed to assist the public in procuring return Bhuriahs at the following rates for 1841:- To Pucheem 4 annas, Kursiang 12 annas, Titalya 1 rupee, with a fee of 1 rupee to the sircar for every twenty coolies provided, and a moiety for half that number.

17. All residents and visitors, subscribers to the "Coolie Charity" or "Charity Hospital Fund," have the privilige of sending their servants to the hospital for medical advice and attendance.

18. Lithographed copies of the Rules, Bye laws, &c., to be had at the Kutcherry at 8 annas each

(Signed)   A. CAMPBELL
Superintendant.

A week before the Wernikes arrived at Darjeeling, an advertisement in the ENGLISHMAN seems to suggest that the place had its normal problems and needs:

AYAH FOR A LADY
Wanted an Ayah for a lady at Darjeeling,
either Portugese, Christian native, or Mussulman
woman. Apply at the Englishman Office.
Tuesday, Dec. 7th, 1841.

Chapter 3

DARJEELING.

What did Darjeeling look like in 1841 when the Wernickes and Stölkes arrived? A general description compiled in 1844 would apply also to 1841 except that there had been more trees but fewer "cottages" and St. Andrew's Church had not been built yet.

The "Darjeeling Guide" for 1845 is an enlightening source of information on all kinds of subjects such as the *"List of Locations and Proprietors."* This list shows a seemingly slow growth of the hill station for whose establishment the *"Ditchers"* (Calcutta citizens) had clamoured for years and heaped abuse on the Government for dilatoriness and unhelpfulness. Yet the Government had actually been cooperative, though rightly cautious, and accepted most suggestions made by the *"Dorjeeling Association"* of prospective settlers.

With allowances made for inaccuracies in the compilation of *"The Guide,"* numbers are disappointing; of the 96 locations marked on the Darjeeling plan (including Lebong and Jalapahar) distributed to 62 applicants, only 20 were by the end of 1844 still the proprietors and original grantees; the rest had changed hands. Sam Smith, renowned editor of the *"Hurkaru"* and one of the chief promoters of the Darjeeling scheme, is recorded as *"Proprietor"* of 26 properties — a blatant case of speculation. Smith must have taken over these plots for sale or seasonal letting. There were other speculators like Sir. T. H. Maddock with 6 properties, and Sir T. E. M. Turton with 5, both members of Government. Col. Lloyd and Dr. Campbell were each content with 3, either for letting or future family extension. Although building was a condition of the lease, the *"Guide"* states under "PRIVATE HOUSES".

"Of these there are already about thirty, principally of wattle and dab; some with iron roofs, but most with bamboo choppers - mere cottages of a better sort. Several pukka houses have lately been built, and three new buildings of this description are in hand this year (1845)"

The list of Europeans of residence is even more disappointing and cannot be complete because the twenty souls or so do not include the Wernickes or the Stölkes.

As for the list of visitors — Darjeeling was not exactly overrun by holiday-makers; in 1842 there had been 42, in 1843 twelve more — 54, and in 1844 just two more — 56!

224 **Expense of Building at Dorjeeling.**

List of Prices proposed to be charged by W. Martin & Co., for Building, &c, at Dorjeeling.

		Rs	as.	
MASONRY.				
Puckha bricks laid in clay,	at	20	0	per 100 ft.
Cutcha bricks laid in clay,	„	17	0	„
Chimnies, puckha bricks, soorkey mortar,	„	28	0	„
PLAISTERING.				
With lime and sand on brick walls,	„	4	0	„
With lime and soorkey,	„	5	0	„
With common sand,	„	1	12	„
With clay on lath walls,	„	3	12	„
Plain cornices with lime and sand,	„	0	8	running ft.
SAND RUBBING.				
With common sand,	„	1	0	per 100 ft.
With lime and sand,	„	1	12	„
WHITE WASHING.				
New brick walls 3 coats,	„	1	6	„
Old „ „ 2 coats,	„	0	12	„
New lath walls 3 coats,	„	1	8	„
Old „ „ 2 coats,	„	0	12	„
COLORING.				
Plain colors,	„	1	8	„
PAINTING.				
In oils common colors 3 coats,	„	8	8	„
„ „ „ 2 coats,	„	6	8	„
„ „ „ 1 coat,	„	4	8	„
FLOORING.				
1¼ inch planks including sleepers,	„	20	0	„
1½ inch „ without sleepers,	„	16	0	„
CIELING.				
1 inch plank, including beams,	„	23	0	„
BAMBOO ROOFING.				
Including scantled rafters, and nailed on,	„	22	0	„
Including round stick rafters put on Lepcha fashion,		17	0	„
Without the rafters,	„	6	8	„
DOORS.				
Panel, including hinges, screws and fixing,	„	1	2	per sqr. ft.
½ panel ½ glass including glass, &c.,	„	1	8	„
All glass, „ „ „	„	1	4	„
Chokets according to sizes „ „	from 5 to	10	0	each
WINDOWS.				
Panel, without fixing, &c.,	at	0	14	per sqr. ft.
½ glass, „ „ „	„	0	12	„
All glass or windows „	„	0	10	„
Ditto, including glass, &c.	„	1	4	„
Shutters, including hinges, &c.,	„	1	0	„
Supplying glass, according to size, from 8 as. to		1	0	per pane

Dorjeeling, 29th Nov. 1842. WILLIAM MARTIN & Co.

N. B. It is to be understood, that at these rates, the bricks are to be made at or near the spot where they are required.—Timber, likewise, for beams, planking, &c., to be had near or on the spot, as carriage for any distance would much enhance these rates. Ornamental painting, and other minor jobs, in proportion as to price.

12.Expense of Building at Darjeeling

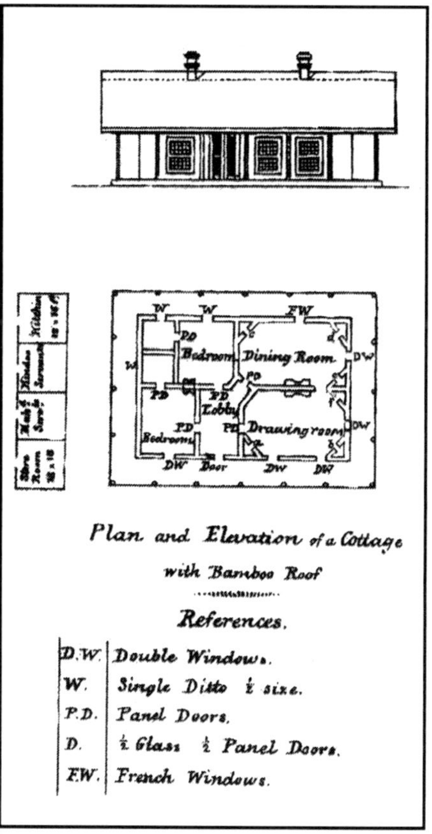
W
W
FW
PD
Bedroom
Dining Room
DW
W
PD
PD
PD
Lobby
PD
PD
Bedroom
Drawing room
DW
DW
Door
DW
DW
Plan and Elevation of a Cottage
with Bamboo Roof
References.
D.W. Double Windows.
W. Single Ditto ½ size.
P.D. Panel Doors.
D. ½ Glass ½ Panel Doors.
F.W. French Windows.

13. Plan of Cottage

But the place was by no means as empty as it sounds, because there were hundreds of local tribal people who had come either to settle in the British enclave, or to hire themselves out as labourers to the Government or to the Government approved contractors, Hepper & Martin. With so many people about, Darjeeling became a natural attraction to any kind of trader as well, and the bazaar seems to have flourished.

This then was the place to which people fled to escape the heat of the Plains of India, and from which they escaped when the cold weather arrived in the hills — the place where Sophie would spend all her life and her children and children's children after her — and all loved it …..

THE DARJEELING PROJECT — 1841

The beginning of the Darjeeling Project is veiled in darkness. It is most probable that Start had previously gone up to Darjeeling to inspect the place and assess the missionary opportunities it was likely to offer. The survey was favourable and Start decided to set up a mission station. The main recommendations were, of course, a healthy climate and the friendly disposition of the Lepcha.

In April 1841 Start and Brother Schulze went to Darjeeling to prepare for the transfer of the missionaries. In June it is reported to Berlin that "a house and land have already been bought." Brother Schulze sends home an enthusiastic description, printed in *"The Bee in the Mission Field"*:

"Darjeeling lies at the foot of the Himalayas whose snow peaks they can see from there. The climate is so cold that in April they are in need of heating; this part of the country is mountainous and wooded. The inhabitants have their own language and are good-natured and peaceable highlanders. Darjeeling itself is a place to which during the hot season many Englishmen go who cannot stand the climate or for recuperation. Brother) Start intends to found there a mission station and Brother Schulze is prepared to remain there; they have also already started to learn the language. This station is specially meant partly for those among us who cannot stand the climate and partly for those who wish to support themselves by their own labour in farming, market gardening or some craft. We are glad of this attempt and hope the Lord will approve of it. And so it appears that your wish to fill the Himalayas with the Gospel is going to be fulfilled. How marvellous are the ways of the Lord!"

Another lyrical report on Darjeeling dates from June 1841:

"The climate is quite temperate, almost cold because of the proximity of the mountains (the snow peaks of the Himalayas shine into their windows!) The station is prettily situated, a house is already there and several more are to be built or purchased; a large piece of arable land is all ready for planting, and the forest is so airy that the whole place is very healthy. During the first year living up there will be rather expensive, because everything is dear, but in the following year the Brethren will produce all food themselves. Regarding the inhabitants, the Lepchas are very independent in their character, not so submissive like the Hindu; they are strong in body and suffer little of illness, indeed, the common illnesses are almost

all unknown. They have an open countenance and are very amiable. The situation of the mission is most delightful to all those who like to be active and diligent,and the more one works here the better one feels. Towards evening high mountains rise in one long chain, all covered in high leafy trees. Towards midnight when the sky is clear one can see in the distance and sky-high the wide snowfields. Towards noon and early morning, overgrown mountains rise high up; the atmosphere is very

14.Bhutias at Breakfast

changeable, but one feels comfortable. We are amid the thunder clouds which come up from between the mountains and fill the gaps; they are numerous but I hear of no damage or fear. Br. Schulze is not likely to recover; it seems that he has a tumour in the brain in which case a cure is hopeless".

The description of the landscape is as true now as it was then, but the reality of the housing situation was rather different from what the Berliners were led to believe and which Sophie Wernicke later remembers with still lingering dismay.

THE MOVE TO DARJEELING — 1841

15. Travelling Wagons

"In the year 1841 we suddenly received orders to move to Darjeeling, and we immediately started our journey in a little boat in which we went to Caragola where Mr. and Mrs. Cave, friends of Start, supplied us with provisions for our journey. From here we went on in horrible ox-carts (two-wheeled carts) for a fortnight. I still today can almost feel the unpleasant pushes and thumps on those bad roads. The nights we spent in tents

which had to be pitched anew every evening. With us were my brother, Missionary Stölke, who actually had received the order to leave behind at Ghazipur his young wife, who had come to India the previous year with Prochnow, but he refused to comply with this unreasonable demand. At Purneah her child became very ill, and we therefore had to remain there for several days but received during this gloomy time much help from Mr. and Mrs. Pringle, the Magistrate of Purneah. On we went — always by this primitive ox-cart via Kishenganj to Punkabari, where we were supposed to take a rest with the natives under the same shelter. The smoke of their fires, the odour from their bodies, and all the noise without which the heathens are unthinkable, made it impossible for us to remain there, particularly because of our little children. We therefore moved on into the bungalow set up for Europeans; as a punishment, however, we had to sack our cook, which made life for us young mothers considerably more difficult. As the real climb into the Himalaya mountains began there, we had to wait for the arrival of our coolies with the dandies (then a simple chair on either side of which was fastened a long pole with a plank for a foot-rest) in which the women were carried the 8,600 feet to Darjeeling; the men had to walk!

One night we rested in a house without roof, windows and doors, something not very agreeable in the middle of the cold winter.

16. Punkabaree

We arrived at Darjeeling on 11 December 1841, but remained here only two days and then descended to Tukvar, about six miles distant from Darjeeling, where nothing had been prepared at all for our arrival. We lived here in a plain Lepcha hut and were not allowed to keep any servants, which meant we had to do every bit of work ourselves; only a cowherd were we permitted to engage. Darjeeling was then a dense jungle without paths, in which lived many wild animals. There was no trace of a village or colony of villas with splendid streets, promenades and electric lighting as we have now. The roaring of leopards and bears and the shrieking of the monkeys which plundered our maize field that had been planted with so much toil, frightened us many a night, for the weakly built hut, whose door was only a thin mat behind which we and our little children slept, offered no *sufficient protection. One evening the whole forest simply swarmed with wolves, and throughout the night the howling of the beasts was so frightening that we hardly closed an eye. When we rather hesitantly left the house in the morning, instead of our five beautiful cows, we only found their skeletons. They had been completely devoured by the wolves. Only the largest bones and horns were left over. This must have been a pack of over a hundred wolves, which, showing their teeth, were surrounding and watching us. Only the unfamiliar sound of shots from our single musket drove away.these eager marauders"*

Sophie Wernicke's reminiscences of her trek to Darjeeling and first impressions of the new hill station are supplemented in some detail by a letter written by Br. Wernicke and Stölke soon after their arrival, dated Darjeeling, 20th January 1842.

"On 14 November we left Patna and on 13 December we arrived here at Tukvar, one mile from Darjeeling. The mountains are something stupendous but immensely fertile. Darjeeling is 7,000 — 8,000 ft. high, Takvar 2,000 ft. lower, completely enclosed by mountains. We live in a house made of mats and bamboo, walls, roof, doors, windows, floor — all of bamboo.

During our travel we had to suffer many dangers and not a little from illness; but we also found on the way a friendly reception from a Christian who showed us much love above all expectation. Lastly, we went across the mighty mountains where wild and dangerous animals have their caves, and where we could not use wheeled transport anymore, and had to go on foot, the women with their small children in their laps being carried in a "dandy." We want to farm here, but first we have to clear away trees, trunks and all has to be removed and burnt in order to prepare the fields. Most is meant to be done with cattle through milk and butter, and therefore several cows have already been purchased with which we believe we shall be able to support ourselves well. The territory was bought by the English three years ago from the King of the Ziebers (?) ((Rajah of Sikkim)) who as nomads never remain long in one place but move on after two or three years. There are four to five tribes: the Lepcha and Batiga and others which we do not know yet. Their language is so different from Hindustani as those from German. The Lepcha appear to be a good people; they are almost white and are very strong, both men and women; they seem to have some kind of divine worship and do not have idols or castes, eat all meats and do not hesitate to eat with us. The English gladly see us settling down here and cultivating the land so that the people join us and accept the Gospel. Therefore, we beg of you to pray for us and that the Lord may put us here as a blessing. A few of the local people understand a little Hindustani with which we can help ourselves and talk to them a little. The people live separated in the forest but are not timid or fearful like the Hindus. Here we never see the sun rise before 8 o'clock, and in the evening it is behind the mountains by 5 o'clock, although it still shines for another two hours. We have already sown all kinds: beans, peas, cabbage, lettuce, etc. We cannot always see Darjeeling, which is 2,0000 ft. higher because clouds are between us. There is no snow or ice here, only sometimes hoar-frost. Yet we always see snow on the highest mountain which is always, summer and winter, covered in eternal snow, but 60 — 80 miles ((actually 40)) away from us and 27,000 ft. high. The soil is so rich that wheat could be sown everywhere; but all is still forest and so thick that one can hardly crawl through it.

Our food is usually rice and dal (a kind of lentil) and meat. Bread is very expensive and inedible. But it will be better in a year when we can prepare everything ourselves. People come to us daily to see how we work; they are talkative and completely independent, their character is more European than Hindustani. The land is cheap: 20 acres can be bought for 150 florins. Cattle can be put out to graze anywhere in the woods."

The withdrawal of the cook and the prohibition of the use of local labour, excepting a cowherd, were again examples of Start's autocratic manner which, however, his missionaries accepted meekly and without complaint. In those days most people knew their station, high or low, and behaved accordingly. Fortunately, however, Start left Darjeeling at the end of 1841, soon after their arrival; Schulze being already familiar with all the arrangements made by him.

It had been Start's custom to spend the cold weather in the plains and the hot season in the hills. He himself could not stand the cold of Darjeeling and knew the difficulties of, for instance, keeping warm (a problem to this day!) but did not hesitate to bring three European families with babies up in freezing weather and put them in a bamboo hut! A Wernicke grandson (Wilfred) has put on record that *"grand mama told me they ….. were the first white family to winter in Darjeeling after the garrison had gone down for the winter."* The climate was considered too tough even for the tough military, but Start thought it was alright for the Wernickes and Stölkes ……

At least Schulze, the Wernickes, Stölkes and Treutlers could breathe freely and try their best without the constant pressure and tension that must have prevailed when Start was about. The few bits of news from Darjeeling still in existence from that time sound relaxed; in particular a long report from Schulze sent in August 1842, giving a full account of the customs of the Lepchas, which would have pleased any anthropologist; it is one of the most complete and earliest descriptions of this tribe:

"*As far as I am able, I now want to write for you something about the country here and its inhabitants. All the mountains around here are only thinly settled. Here and there one sees on the mountain slopes patches of cereals with singly lightly built houses. These houses normally do not last longer than 3 - 4 years, and that is long enough for these highlanders as they do not remain longer in one place. After three years they find themselves another spot and cut down the forest. They do this towards the end of the dry season in the months of January, February, March. All tree trunks are left lying wherever they fall, and since it never rains and the sun is warm, everything dries up and withers. Shortly before the beginning of the rainy season at the end of March beginning of April, all the cut wood is burnt, and whatever remains of the thick trunks after the great fire is collected into one big pile and burnt again, for there is no lack of wood. The stumps remain in the ground. Then when the rainy season comes and the large amount of ashes and the ground have been thoroughly wetted, the patch is sown. In the following months till September, it rains a great deal, almost daily, yet it is not cold; the soil, well-manured with ashes, grows Turkish wheat, rice and other cereals to the height of a man. At the harvest, the straw is left standing in the field and is burnt in the following year, shortly before the rainy season, and then sown. In this manner, it is done one or two years; but then it is thought better to cut down a new patch of forest, because the harvest will be richer. There are no barns, but large, round pits in the ground; these are lined, sides and bottom, with large broad leaves and then the cereals are poured into them after they have been cleaned and dried in the sun. And so, the cereals lie safe from rats, of which there are rather many about. According to need, one pit is opened after the other. The cereals and all fruit keep well in the pits, since from the end of October until the beginning of March it does not rain at all, or only very little. There are no fruit trees or vines, apart from a kind of apple, though sour like crab apples. At Tukvar, lying 1,500 ft. lower and being warmer, the peach trees blossom already at the beginning of February. Moreover, there are some nuts, lilac, oranges and some species of wild figs and berries, but all not very sweet — and also a kind of wild grape. In the nearer neighbourhood live several different tribes. The one among which we live and whose language we are trying to learn, call themselves "Rong;" but the other tribes call themselves "Lepcha." The Rong people are, character-wise, the best. They usually keep in their houses only goats, chickens, and pigs — seldom cattle. They are very cheerful, neither warlike nor thieving; they rarely quarrel with each other, are shy and modest like children. Some, however, are already very spoilt* owing to being long with the people who have come up from the Plains, and set a bad example. Through practice from early childhood, they are strong carriers, for there are no animals to pull or carry, and they have to carry themselves building material, cereals or wood for fuel. They are very skilled at plaiting baskets, hats, umbrellas, blankets, swings and all sorts of vessels of different kinds of bamboo which are found here. The walls, floors and ceilings of their houses are usually plaited bamboo. The women spin cotton on spindles. Their usual dress is a wide, long jacket of raw cotton (red or blue at times) and over the waist, round the body, is a piece of cloth which goes down over the men's knees, but reaches the women's feet. When it is very warm and one works, the men go almost naked, with only a loin cloth around the waist. All walk barefoot throughout the year, most of them without a head covering. They wear their hair long, which some house-fathers at times plait into a pigtail hanging behind, or they cut it off. Earrings and bangles of silver and metal, necklaces and strings, in particular, are customary with women. The men carry on the side from youth in a wooden sheath, a very strong knife, shorter or longer, up to 3/4 ell long, which they use in the forest like an axe, and with which they most skilfully carry out all manner of work. They also often have with them their bow, 3 1/2 ell long, and clay bullets in a bag or arrows in a kind of quiver, and will hit birds, which they eat."

The next letter was written by Br. Stölke at Takvar in May 1843. Its calm is puzzling and without the slightest hint at any disagreement with Start and impending doom. It is, of course, possible that the editor of *"The Bee in the Mission Field"* had printed only the *"honey"* the *"bee"* had collected and ignored, or even avoided, less *"sweet"* news:

"This is a very healthy part of the country and we all keep very well. We can already earn enough so that we do not need any more support. But it is very difficult to work among the people because they have so many languages. In these mountains live Lepcha, Parbusia, Butiga, Limba, Bengalen, Chinese and Hindu; also in their features they differ so that one can immediately recognise to which nation they belong. Also every nation has its own religion. Some pray to trees, others worship stones, animals, sun, moon, etc. Of the living God they know nothing, engage in magic, especially the Lepcha. We sowed three bushels of wheat and barley, and had been very hopeful, but on 15th April, on a quiet Sabbath, came a gale with hail the size of chickens' eggs, and smashed it all, cereals and garden fruit. We kiss the love-rod (Liebesrute) of the Lord for he helps in other ways. We stand alone here, but the Word of the Lord "I am with you all days" is our comfort, and resuscitates our hearts."

Dates and statements during 1842 — 43 are somewhat contradictory and confusing, so that it is not easy to reconstruct the chain of events. Did the *"bombshell"* of expulsion fall before the May letter was written or after? Life cannot have run very smoothly, as may be guessed from what happened next, according to Great-grandmother Wernicke's *"Memoires."*

Sophie Wernicke remembers:

"Our position got even worse in 1843 when Start withdrew his hand from us completely, saying he had run out of money. And we were there now without any means, among alien tribes (chiefly Nepali) whose customs and language we did not know sufficiently, and were dependent entirely on the work of our hands. We begged Mr. Start to leave us at least the land around Takvar which we had cleared with the sweat of our brows, but his hard-heartedness went so far as to refuse us even this as he wanted to keep Tukvar for himself. We could do nothing else but leave Tukvar and settle a little higher up the mountain. We had, of course, to start from scratch to clear the impenetrable jungle in order to make fields and gardens and cultivate them. We also built for ourselves, with our own hands, three pretty houses, one for each family, Missionary Treutler having arrived in the meantime after having heard that the climate was healthier.

We made our living by the sale of self-grown potatoes and some fruits and vegetables. One turned into a baker, the other slaughtered pigs, smoked ham, sausages etc., and I myself prepared butter and cheese which products we sold to the Europeans coming to Darjeeling. Due to the great physical efforts, we all fell very ill again, especially my dear husband, who was bedridden for over a month, which very much depressed us. It also pained us that by this way of living, our real profession was completely neglected. But my husband said: 'We have come out as missionaries, and missionaries we want to remain.' For that reason we wrote to Pastor Prochnow who was stationed at Koteghar, and requested to be taken back into the Gossner Mission and to support us with the necessary means. But this last hope also failed, and since then we have not heard again of the other "siblings," their lives and activities."

Brother Joachim Stölke had a few rather amazing details to add to this account of the abrupt parting of the ways. Months after the event, on 15th September 1844, he reports to the Gossner Mission:

"Mr. Start has withdrawn his hand from us and has left us to ourselves. We had to buy of him everything, and had to pay 6% interest on Rs. 2,000. Then we had to buy a new piece of land 11/2 hours away from Darjeeling from the (East

India) Company which will be taxed after four years. That is the reason why we work very much and cannot dedicate ourselves to the service of the Gospel among the heathen as much as we would wish. But we hope it will soon be better by getting known better to the people, and the natives now gather at certain places in the English territory. We also have ample opportunity to talk with them, since the road passes right in front of our door, whereby we meet them and can tell them of the salvation which is Jesus, as also the people we have with us, servants and workers". Start's severance of all connection with the Darjeeling Moravians in such an unpleasant manner naturally poses the question: Why did he do it? After all, by bringing these young and completely inexperienced people out to India, he thereby had taken upon himself a considerable responsibility. He knew where he was bringing them, and that they were ignorant of everything they ought to have known: the climate, the languages, Indian habits and customs and, in general, the Indian cultural background so essential in the work they were meant to carry out. Apparently, he also made them leave the Gossner Mission, under whose auspices they had gone to India, and made them members of his private mission so that he became their sole authority and director of their activities. The fact that he never joined other missions, though there were many opportunities, but insisted on his own enterprise is already indicative of a certain arrogance. He considered the work of other missionary societies so unsatisfactory that he decided to run his own show.

Already in the first three years of this German contingent, Start had displayed somewhat autocratic tendencies by pushing the young people from one place to another without consultation or explanation, showing no consideration or sympathy with their conditions. Sick and dying children were no concern of his, and the disastrous effects of the weather on "his" missionaries did not bother him. He pushed them about, like pieces on some missionary chess board.

Maybe Start had miscalculated the time it would take for the Moravians to become self-supporting, and felt annoyed that he still had to finance them after five years; but he only had himself to blame for failing to take into account the difficulties newcomers to India had to cope with. He had actually made the same mistake as the other unsuccessful missions who had brought out their "agents" unprepared for their work, and were forced to close down their stations for lack of success: no conversions!

Start's main complaint, no doubt, had been the fact that in two years at Darjeeling not a single heathen had been converted — no baptisms! But how could they have achieved anything without even a basic vocabulary to conduct a most elementary theological discussion? Since they were unable to speak the local languages, they had to read from a tract in the bazaar early in the morning to the astonishment and entertainment of the shoppers — a sermon in pidgin Lepcha can be nothing but amusing. Start had had no patience with other missions and missionaries, and he quite obviously also lacked the two qualities his "agents" were meant to preach: charity and compassion. How else could he throw out families, with their small children, to fend for themselves? The claim that he had run out of money is hardly credible, since he had sufficient means to take over the whole station of the Baptist Missionary Society at Patna in 1849.

Start seems to have compounded his unreasonableness by sending highly critical reports on "his" missionaries to Berlin, or their representative, Pastor Prochnow in India, on their ineffectiveness and inefficiency, in consequence of which his throw-outs were refused re-entry into the Gossner Mission.

There is still another possible explanation for the final separation — Start's strong Baptist views. Our invaluable informant on the mission field, the Rev. W. Buyers, gave a lucid description of the situation. He observed:

"These German missionaries in Mr. Start's connexion, are not generally considered to be under any engagement, either expressed or understood, to remain with him permanently, or to preach his peculiar views. In fact, some of them do not seem to have been aware, when they joined him, that he held sentiments at all different from what are usual among evangelical Churches. This subsequently led to some uneasiness in the minds of several of them, as they seemed to think, that while he did not in the least interfere with their liberty of conscience, he was not a little disappointed to find, that they had not fallen more readily in with is sentiments. While some of them also, were able to go on comfortably, with the self-supporting plan, others felt, that engaging so much in secular business, did not at all comport with their usefulness as missionaries, in a country where studious, as well as active habits, are so much required, as in India."

This described succinctly the plight of the Darjeeling missionaries. The fact that Wernickes (and Stölkes?) joined the Church of England — the church Start had left — seems to confirm the assumption that the Baptist dogma had not appealed to them.

And so it happened that the Wernickes and Stölkes, who had come to India to save the souls of the heathen, suddenly found that they had to save their own souls and bodies to keep the two together. There have been authors who have tried to insinuate that these missionaries had abandoned their work for more lucrative employment with a hint at betrayal of their trust; nothing could be farther from the truth. It must be clearly put on record that they had been abandoned by their promoters! It must also be said that their removal from the "mission field" was a blessing in disguise for all concerned as well as for Darjeeling. By the simplicity of their life-style, their hard work and their fairness of dealing with all those who came in contact with them, they preached a more convincing sermon than many words could have done.

1844

By 1st January 1844 Wernicke, Stölke and Treutler are already reported to "have bought their own piece of land from the Government between Darjeeling and Tukvar, because Mr. Start has kept Tukvar for himself; they intend to carry on by themselves with ease and maintain the Mission without support — favoured by the position of the site. As Simla and Kotghar lie at the western end of the Himalayas, so Darjeeling at the eastern. The brethren there are well." In September a letter with a story of success and satisfaction reaches Berlin:

"Inwardly the Lord blesses us so that we cannot complain. Our place, which we have called "Gnadenberg" (Mount Grace) is very healthy, not so cold as high-up Darjeeling, and not so warm as low-down Tukvar, so that the doctor in Darjeeling sends us the sick who soon enough recover. They also participate in our morning and evening worship. At first we had a captain with family with us who was much edified. Br. Wernicke has been instructing a twelve year old girl for the last seven months, whom we shall soon baptise. Our house, 50 ft. long and 20 broad, with four rooms, is so big that we can easily take in such families. The soil is good and richly repays our labour so that we have already repaid Mr. Start Rs. 500."

There are no records for the period 1844 — Oct. 1846 when Gnadenberg was abandoned. It must be assumed that a certain routine had been established and nothing noteworthy happened that would be of interest to "The Bee." The reason given for the move is that they were too far away from Darjeeling for their mission work. There is, however, a passage in Sophie Wernicke's reminiscences which might fit in here, because it mentions a move to Darjeeling, but somehow her facts cannot be accommodated with the circumstances described by her, for they did not move to the town in 1844 and in 1846 they were not as badly off as she makes out. It looks like a mix-up of memories — after all, she was 85 when she told her story — unless something had gone wrong at Gnadenberg and Br. Stölke preferred not to mention it.

This is Sophie's tale:

"*In our distress we then turned to the clergyman of the Church of England in Darjeeling, and he advised us to sell our little houses, move up to Darjeeling and start burning bricks and cutting wood. These things were at that time very much in demand by the English who had recognised Darjeeling as one of the most conveniently and most beautifully situated spas in India, and wished to build villas here. Although this suggestion did not quite correspond to our requirements, we accepted it — what else could we have done?*"

Whatever the motives, the final transfer into Darjeeling took place, and Br. Stölke could send some encouraging news, seven months later, to "The Bee." On 26 May 1847 he wrote:

"*We gave up our Gnadenberg in October of last year because we were too far away, and now have chosen for us a place near Darjeeling where we have more opportunity to proclaim God's word and distribute tracts, because there we are daily much more surrounded by all classes of the people. Already now God's word is more frequently asked for. Also the translation of the Gospel of St. Matthew into the Lepcha language is complete, which we now distribute and give to those who can read, the Chokas, Lepchas and Nepalis. To be sure, the people who assemble here are bad and spoilt, but the Lord can save even the most spoilt sinner. But one does not see here so many idols and idlers. Most of them try to earn their bread by work.*"

We (Wernicke, Treutler and I) are all keeping well, thanks be to God, and we can well exist without support, so that we have passed on the Rs. 300 you have sent us to the Brethren in R who have greater need of it.

In order to refresh and strengthen ourselves, we meet every Wednesday morning at 10 o'clock with Br. Start and Niebel in Br. Start's chapel for prayer, singing and Bible meditation, which serves us as edification and encouragement. Please remember us at that hour so that our common prayer may come before the Lord. Roman Catholics are also here, and a convent where children are being educated. It looks as if Darjeeling will grow immensely; much building takes place annually, and it is visited by many patients from all over India."

The above letter makes it quite clear that the first generation of "Moravians" had not given up their missionary activities when leaving Tukvar. Sophie Wernicke even adds some details of their increased efforts after their move to Darjeeling:

"*After we had once more founded a new homestead, we built with our own hands in the bazaar a small chapel and school, with a few rooms for the admission of sick brethren. Here was held a meeting for worship every Sunday, early at 8 o'clock for our labourers, and during the week children received lessons."*

In this connection Sophie's answer to the question whether the mission work had achieved anything at all is of interest:

"Eternity may decide. My husband baptised one sole Nepali, the other Brethren, nobody. For the Mission too the saying is valid 'You cannot serve two masters.' For if you depend on earning your daily bread by your own hands, undoubtedly the missionary profession must be neglected."

It is gratifying to read that Start and his missionaries were still on speaking terms, in spite of the uncharitable treatment they had been given. They even met once a week for prayer and Bible study at Start's chapel, which had been built at the cantonment at Jalapahar, chiefly for the benefit of the English soldiers. But the group of three (Wernicke, Stölke and Treutler) had shrunk to two. When Treutler was asked to join the school work, he said that "*he had been thrown out of the Mission and, therefore, did not want to have anything to do with it anymore, but henceforth work for himself.*" (which he seems to have done with great success).

17. Darjeeling circa 1855-60

WHAT THEY KNEW OF THE "MORAVIANS" IN 1849

The General Postmaster, William Tayler, spent some months at Darjeeling in 1849. At the end of the description of his stay, he listed all the pleasant people in the place, for instance:

"There was a Roman Catholic priest whose acquaintance I was glad to make; and several German missionaries, good men, who, finding their special missions hopeless, had taken to making sausages."

Plate 18. Bungalow near Thieve's Corner

THE BENGAL HURKARU AND INDIA GAZETTE
NOVEMBER 28th , 1849

Private letters from Darjeeling state that in consequence of Dr .Campbell and Dr. Hooker having proceeded further into the Sikim territory than the Raja considered consistent with the existing treaty, they had been arrested and detained, and that military demonstrations had been made on both sides, which had caused much uneasiness at Darjeeling

"We hear that the 14th N.I., now at Berhampore, are under orders for the Sikim frontier, and that six mountain guns are to follow forthwith - to bring the Raja to account for his incarceration of Drs. Campbell and Hooker."

*"**Darjeeling, 22nd November 3 A.M.** You will, I dare say, be surprrised at seeing my letter dated at 3 o'clock in the morning. You probably heard that the station has been in a commotion lately, in consequence of the Sikim Raja having detained Dr. Campbell. Several very strange reports have been in circulation the last two days, and we heard last night that a guard of Sepoys have been ordered to keep walking round the station all night, relieving each other by turns, there is talk of the Sikim people coming to Darjeeling. We went to bed as usual last night, at a little after ten o'clock, thinking that it was merely an invention of the natives, and that we were quite safe; but about half past eleven we were aroused by the station Staff Officer, Captain Nicolson, calling out at the door to us to dress immediately and be in readiness to start with a guard of Sepoys which would be sent to conduct us to a place of safety should it be necessary for us to leave our house, which he thought likely. You may imagine our alarm at this. We have further heard that nine hundred rupees worth of rice has been collected by the Sikim people; some of it is at Adulpore and some at the Rungeet. As we are afraid to go to bed in case of falling asleep, I thought I may as well spend the time in writing to you. The European Invalid soldiers, of the depot here, have received orders to be in readiness all night in case of their services being required, and that they have had ten rounds of ammunition served out to them. Every noise we hear makes me start and tremble. We sent for Mr. W. at about twelve o'clock, and he is with us still for we are afraid to be left. Every sound we hear we think it is the guard come to escort us to Capt. Byng's house. The Invalids here are under orders to be sent to Dinapore, but those who are able to work were to be detained at Darjeeling to guard the treasury in case of any disturbance. There are chowkidars screaming out now and then all over the station. All this disturbance has been occasioned by Dr. Campbell going further than he ought to have done, and it seems that the Sikim people are very much enraged by the manner in which Dr. Campbell treated an*

Ambassador sent by the Sikim Raja to him. I am so nervous and cold I hardly know what I am writing. We have wished ourselves in Calcutta a hundred times at least during the night, I think you will say, when you read this, that we have some cause for alarm".

"There is a report that some of the Sikim people are on their way from the Rungeet, cutting the jungle as they come along. We have heard that Captain Byng (Officiating Superintendant) has put men to guard some part of the supplies of rice collected for the Sikim people, at which they will be very much enraged. If they should come into Darjeeling, we should all be starved out I fancy. This is a pleasant prospect, especially as we must stay where we are, as the roads are not safe for ladies to travel on just now. If this had occurred a few days later, the European troops would not have been here, as I believe they were to have started on the 26th. It is now past 4 A.M. and nothing has as yet happened; but a report says, that the Sikim army is on this side of the Rungeet, which I hope and trust may not be true, but we do not feel secure enough to retire to rest, though as you may suppose, we are very much in want of it as we have only had one hours rest."

" 9A.M. At five o'clock we were so tired of watching that we went to lie down and rest, and Mr. W. - promised to watch till daylight. We have seen several persons this morning and I am grieved to say there is no better news. The enemy it appears are more likely to arrive tonight than they were last evening. We are now going to the Byngs to make some arrangement, if we can, to escape to Punkabarree. There is no secure place here we fear. I hope this may reach you safely and trust in God that all may yet go well. I hear troops are coming in from Dinapore, but they are not expected for a fortnight or three weeks, and a great deal of mischief may be done before that time. We all feel very tired after having been up all night, and most likely may have to do so again tonight. Mr. Hodgson has armed all his servants, and we have heard that the sepoys do not know how to handle a musket, but I cannot say whether this is true or not. we have heard that the Bhaugulpore Hill Rangers are expected here also, but not for some time yet.

Captain Byng (the commandant) and Captain Nicolson (the Station staff) have just been here and said they strongly advised us to move into Captain Samler's house, the one the O'Shaughnessys occupied, and also the one Mr. Cathcart occupied as they are close together and can be protected by the military. Poor Captain Nicolson looks very much fagged. Captain Sayers and Lieut. Freeman are going on the road leading to the Rungeet to see if they can see any signs of the enemy. The natives have been doing their best to frighten us out of our lives today. If I have anything new to tell, I will write again tomorrow."

DISTURBANCES IN DARJEELING — BROTHER STÖLKE REPORTS ON UPROAR, ASSAULTS AND ATROCITIES

15th December 1849, Bro. Stölke writes from Darjeeling. Just as he was about to set up a school, suddenly disturbances have arisen. *"It happened that an English magistrate and others travelled to the King of Sikkim, on whose land and territory they dwell, as they must do every year. But the King has taken them prisoner, thrown them into jail and grossly maltreated them; indeed it was first reported that they had been murdered by the natives. The entire Lepcha people were in uproar and threatened to attack Darjeeling, to murder, set alight and burn. Everyone took refuge and left their houses empty. In reply the army, black and white soldiers, were mustered, gun positions were established and the attack was awaited — but it never came. Envoys were sent to the king to say, that if he did not free the prisoners and return them, words would be replaced by the sword. So he let them go and sent them back. But what will happen further with him we do not know, but still many troops are assembling. At first the Brethren too fled but soon returned to their houses. The army commander reassured them and promised them that they would be given an immediate warning, if there was any danger. You can imagine their feelings in a country surrounded on all sides by hostile natives, on the West Nepal, to the North Sikkim, in the East Bhutan, and only one way to the Plains lying open. These peoples all lie deep in a deathly slumber. Tibet and China are closed and no man dares enter. Yet from all these people some come to Darjeeling and so it may be that one or other of them will take the Word back with them to their own country."*

It was this news item that was accompanied by an illustration of the hill station of Darjeeling, the earliest picture which gives a more or less correct idea of the layout of the place; Observatory Hill, St. Andrew's Church and Col. Lloyd's bungalow below the church are clearly recognisable.

1854 - A SCHOOL

In 1854 the *"Bee"* joyfully reported that:

"The Lord's work has been renewed in Darjeeling. The Bros. Wernicke and Stölke have built a fine school house, which will serve as a church every Sunday. From the first of May a school for heathen boys has been started. Bro. Wernicke has several Christians from Bettiah (?) in his employment, and three unbelievers, an old Hindu and two young Nepalese, who wish to become Christians, are being prepared for baptism."

This must be the building which Sophie mentions in greater detail:

"*After we had now once again established a new domestic way of life, we built with our own hands a small chapel and school by the bazaar with a few small rooms for the reception of sick Brethren. So now early every Sunday here at 8 o'clock the Lord's service was held, mainly for our workers, and during the week instruction was given to the children. My brother joined in with this missionary work while Mr. Treutler said that he had been driven out of the Mission and so did not want anything more to do with it, but from now on was going to work for himself*"

There appears to be some confusion regarding the beginning of Lepcha education at Darjeeling. Recent authors write that:

"*To the Rev. William Start, a Baptist, is accorded the honour of being the earliest labourer in the field, for it was he who opened, as far back as 1841, using his private means, the first school for Lepchas. This is what one can understand about the establishment of a native school (at Tukvar).*" [Dick Dewar]

Alas, this is a misunderstanding. The Tukvar Mission, as it is also sometimes called, was the home of the German missionaries with their families, whose two main occupations were learning the Lepcha language and clearing the jungle around Tukvar to enable them to grow their own food. There was neither room nor time to run a school as well. Their "educational activity" consisted of going to the bazaar early in the morning and reading some missionary tract to their Lepcha audiences. But it was also at Tukvar that C. G. Niebel translated several books of the Bible into Lepcha, and generally speaking, the place was a centre of translation work which eventually became the basis of Lepcha education. That the response to the educational facilities offered was very poor, becomes apparent from Brother Stölke's description of the fate of the school that had been built with so much toil, and opened in 1854 with so much hope:

"*Darjeeling, 30th May, 1858 ….. The school which we had started had to be given up since the heathen did not want to send their children. Then the Government began a school with one English and one Indian teacher, without all religion, that is to say without Christianity (they could practise their heathen religion): although at first 50 — 60 children had been promised, never more than 15 or 16 arrived, and therefore after 1 1/2 years the English teacher was sent away and only the Indian remained, and the school is in our house. The heathen do not want to recognise what is useful to them. God who calls the hearts of all men ("Herzenskündiger") and who has pity on all heathen will let His time come for them. What we fear is that before long the Nepalis will push us aside: we are in the hands of this people as they surround us on all sides. We can only pray for a general peace for ourselves and our country, and it seems that the English always win the victory though often with much loss .....*"

So much for the beginning of "Lepcha education" .....

1857

The Mutiny of 1857 never reached Darjeeling, but people there were well aware of what was happening in the Plains and took proper precautions as described in a letter by Br. Stölke to a friend a year after the outbreak of the troubles, in May 1858:

"Concerning ourselves, we are all still alive, thanks be to the Lord, though we had to go through some distress and trouble and trials of all kinds, especially last year [1857] when the Lord's cup of wrath was poured out over India and many thousands of whites and blacks had to give up their lives, on account of Sin. However, it now seems to become quiet though the whole country is still rebellious, and in general, unsafe for Europeans to travel. At the entrance to our station were made strong fortifications. Many of the rebels have been caught and were hanged. Six such murderers had to mount the scaffold and "decorate" the gallows. The chief murderer of the lieutenant who was my neighbour, has not yet been found. Many English soldiers are still to come to the assistance of this country. When there is quiet again and the rebellion has come to an end, there will be hope for us that the Lord's word will find acceptance among those who till now have resisted Him ....."

Sophie Wernicke had her own memories of those fearful months:

"During the Indian rebellion in 1857, we were in great anxiety when all the horrible news of the frightful tortures and massacres of the English by the natives reached us. For the sake of security we had to leave our house, as it was too secluded and remote, and in the hour of danger would not have given us sufficient protection; we therefore moved to the other Europeans who live here. By the grace of God, however, we were spared all evil, although the native soldiers stationed at Darjeeling, had already decided to kill all whites. At one of their revolutionary meetings, they were all arrested and taken prisoners. Only one lieutenant, who had come to Darjeeling for recuperation and had been happy that he had escaped the fate of his comrades who had all been murdered at Cawnpore, was attacked in his house whilst he was asleep, and killed in a ghastly manner.

This lieutenant was a neighbour of Br. Stölke, and his murderer was caught in no time. It was established that the murder was not connected with the Mutiny but had been a plain case of robbery.

19. The Chief of the Murderers of Lieut.Whish, from a photograph.

THE MURDER OF LIEUTENANT WHISH.

Iᴛ will be recollected that one of the earliest atrocities of the mutineers in India we had to record was the murder of the above officer, thus related in a letter from Darjeeling, dated 18th June:—

Lieutenant Whish was found murdered in his own house on the morning of the 16th instant, but as yet it is unknown by whom ; though strong suspicions rest on his own servants, who were all Bhootias. They are now in close confinement. The deed was done apparently merely to get his money—a certain sum, which it was well known he had in the house, was taken out of one of his trunks, found broken open ; a pair of pistols also were taken away.—*Bengal Hurkaru, June* 23.

The villain who was the chief in this atrocity has since been hanged ; but the day before his execution a photograph was taken of him, a copy of which has since been forwarded to us by a Correspondent from Calcutta, and is engraved above.

Chapter 4

SCHOOLING

Joachim Stölke appears to have done well enough to afford sending his two boys to St. Paul's School. But his economic progress did not stop him from taking a continued interest in the mission work, as he indicates in his letter of June 7, 1860:

"For some time now I should have written from our Himalayan mountains. Oh! If only I could write that Satan's bulwark has been overcome like in some other places where our Brethren work. But no trace of awakening is noticeable, which I deplore with sadness. People hear the Word, often with joy, which is proclaimed to them. Of all classes and social standing, they also take books from us, but that is all.

What concerns us in particular I can say, praise the Lord, all of us are healthy and well. My two sons are in Calcutta at St. Paul's School. The eldest is there in his second year. My wife accompanied him down and returned from the journey to our mountains healthy and well after three months. He wants to study theology in order to train as a missionary and preacher, for which the Lord may give him strength. He has a good disposition and makes gratifying progress, and the Rector writes of him: 'The good seed that has been sown at the home of his parents brings forth good fruit.' The second son also went there this year. He does not know yet what he wants to become. They cost me a great deal at this school. All the daughters I still have with me. They are all grown up and give me much joy, and help their mother in the house.

Brother Wernicke is still suffering (gout) and can do nothing. His three sons are also at the school in Calcutta, the last one since February. He has four daughters at home, the youngest being 1 1/2 years old."

It was about this time that Andreas Wernicke's health rapidly deteriorated. He had been suffering severely from gout since the beginning of the 1850's to the extent that he was too incapacitated to attend to his work. Sophie remembers with sorrow how:

"The clouds of adversity gathered even more thickly, for my dear husband became so heavily afflicted with rheumatism and gout that he became quite incapable of doing any work, and at the same time he developed very ugly ulcers around his hips and on a foot. Often he was away for months at a time, seeking relief at the Mineral Spring some 5 English miles from here, but unfortunately he

usually returned with very little in way of more strength. Now I had not only to care for my six children but to supervise all his work. In those days there also occurred all the frontier disturbances with Sikkim, a little state between Nepal and Bhutan, which often threatened to wipe out Darjeeling and all its inhabitants. This served to increase our cares and tension."

The border troubles with Sikkim went back to the imprisonment of Dr. Campbell and Dr. Hooker in 1849. As a punishment, the British Government annexed 640 sq. miles of the Rajah's territory and stopped his annual payment of Rs. 6,000. There was plunder and kidnapping of British subjects in ever increasing numbers: An ultimatum to hand over the victims and the criminals was ignored, and Dr. Campbell unsuccessfully invaded Sikkim. It was then that wild rumours circulated of thousands of warriors descending from Sikkim and Bhutan to fall upon Darjeeling. However, not a single soldier made his appearance, and the Rajah was forced to sue for peace and make the Treaty of Tumlong in 1861, and British relations with Sikkim were again normalised.

Although Andreas Wernicke was no doubt in a bad way and not very mobile, he was still able to take an active interest in what was going on around him. One of his main concerns was the education of his sons whom he had sent, at great expense, to a school, Doveton College, in Calcutta. Fortunately, some, or all his letters to the boys, have been preserved and allow a glimpse at an outstandingly kind man, who pours all his affection for his children into warm words of comfort, support, advice and trust. Frank Warwick (Wernicke before WW1 — the patriotic Wernickes anglicised their name during the war) has recorded his grandfather's correspondence for the benefit of later generations, and all those who want to know their "roots." Frank writes:

"In 1860 my father, 18, his brothers Fred, 16, and Samuel, 12, were sent to Calcutta to Doveton College for further education. There are several letters written during the next 2 years written by their father which serve to illustrate the anxieties of parents separated from their children and the loneliness and homesickness of the boys, as well as giving glimpses into their lives. None of these letters sent by post were in envelopes. Double sheets of thin paper were used, one side being left blank for the address. The letter was folded and tucked into itself. Along with the address the word "Stamped" was written as an extra precaution against the removal of the stamp before the post-mark, date and place were added. This was a common form of pilfering especially for higher denominations. The absence of envelopes reflected the need for extreme economy, which the grandparents had to exercise."

Extracts from letters from their father to Andrew and Fred while at Doveton College.

January 11th, 1860 to Andrew

"God keep you all well and bring you safely to Calcutta, that is our one prayer. From your letter it seems as if you were most grieved ..... should the climate not agree with you, you should come up at once. Keep up your spirits and be not sad if thoughts come of home. Amuse yourself and try to overcome that. Remember that going down can be of great importance to your life. You should therefore think of it because I am very weak and do not know what may please the Lord ..... My dear Fred, your brother is not so sad; that is good."

February 6th, 1860

"Indeed, my dear child, it is a great blessing that the Lord has brought you safely to Calcutta and that you all enjoy good health. We join with you in giving thanks to our Heavenly Father and pray to Him that He may continue with His Grace towards you and us ..... . Now my dear Andrew, you are the eldest. Try and be a pattern for your younger brothers. Agree all nicely together and love each other. And my dear Andrew, I was glad to hear you will assist both your brothers. That is right. Do it in humility and patience. You did it indeed very good that you bought Fred a suit of dark cloth. It has pleased me and dear Mama very much. Our two cows cost Rs. 40 with their two calves and another one I bought with a calf for Rs. 6 annas 8."

February 9th, 1860 to Andrew

"Do not overwork yourself: be never sad, have happy spirits and try to keep up your brother Fred, who seems to suffer He is sad and in very low spirits."

Same date to Fred

"You mention you do not feel so well and suffer loose bowels. I hope by this time you are well and strong again. I give you permission to buy a ball but take care and do not exhaust yourself in playing. You know from that you get loose bowels. Rather rest but a ball you get and pay it from the money I sent you and pay for everything you take from Mr. Pierse [Peisie?]. You must let me know when your money is spent but take care at the same time how you spend it as it is hard for us to get it."

<u>March 21st, 1860 to Andrew</u>

"I am thinking so much of you all as it is of so great importance that you all learn well, that you should like it and that none of you should feel it a burden to be away from us. .... if you were to return as you have gone down to school fit for nothing whereas now in the world none of the Europeans can get on well without it. It is always, dear Andrew, my greatest desire to you all, that you should learn well, redeem the time, that is to say <u>apply the time to learning</u> and not idle it away and more so, if people have not that, what many others have, as honour and riches and then not to have knowledge and learning. Learning is everything and more than money. <u>Do you hear all my dear children</u> but remember that I have always said to you 'Above all whatever you do, do in the name of our Lord Jesus' ..... I shall leave off with these words. Reflect of what I have written to you. God our Father bless you in body and spirit and keep you all in health. PS We have not many customers."

<u>May 1860, to Andrew</u>

"We are so sorry that Fred is suffering from his ear. My dear Fred, bear it patiently. When the cold weather sets in you shall come home. That is a great thing that your bowels are right. Take great care of yourself .... last night our goods reached us and the girls were so happy to unpack because of the toys you sent for them. They are very much pleased for them. Little Gusta fights hard for hers and she is so amused, it is delightful to watch her. Andrew said he would send some old cloth for Bearer, also that he would return his gun. Nothing of them is come. We suppose he has not sent any but the two old blankets in the basket and the box with the crockery. Dear Mama and I are weak though Mama is always working hard. ..... The station is very empty this year and our sale is only a little. The weather is still cool and the cutback [cuckoo?] here and there. We have more than one about us now."

<u>May 31st, 1860 to Andrew</u>

"Dear Mama was very ill a few days ago and I was obliged to call in the Doctor and after taking some medicines I am glad to say she is better again. Your sisters have all been very well. Today dear Emma was obliged to take some castor oil. They all four went down to their Aunt for her birthday yesterday [Dorothea Sophie W. m. Joachim Stölke] and I think Emma took too much cake, which made her sick. I am pretty well. I am sorry you lost two rupees. You will have received the small draft for Rs. 12. Do not cash it before you require it. Dear Samuel, you must write oftener. We get very seldom letters from you. That will not improve you in letter

writing. Tomorrow there will be an Exhibition in the Assembly Rooms of all kinds of flowers, also of jungly flowers and plants. I hear the new baker with his sweetmeats also and the Butchers will bring their things for show and try to get the price. Dr. Jerden will also show what he has gathered and give a lecture on all."

Feb. 17th, 1861 to Andrew

"I am sorry you are troubled in your mind. If it is over work, do not work too hard and do not read at all until you have got over this disease. Take my advice, never sit up late but go to bed every evening at nine o'clock. .... Should your disease be of another kind, you know that Jesus our Lord has died for sinners and that if we are accused in our mind that we are lost, that is not true. Jesus died for sinners, sinners we are, sinners we will be as long as we live, Satan will accuse the children, then we have to look up to Jesus who knows that we are weak. Keep faith. Remember our forefathers and how weak they were, but they did not despair but confessed their sins and kept faith in him."

May 17th, 1861 to Andrew

"In one of your letters you asked me to send you the flute. I am sorry to say it is so bad that it could be of no use to you, and then I do not think your chest is strong enough to play it; rather if you like to learn any music I think the fiddle is best for you. My brother also had a fancy to play and had a horn, by which he ruined his health altogether, so let me advise you to take care. If you like to have a fiddle you shall have it. How is your and Sam's cloth [clothes]? Are you in want of anything? Ask Mr Pecise [?] for everything as I have sent him plenty of money. I have ordered Mr. P. to give Fred Rs. 150 for his way up. He has to bring with him a large supply of goods. When he comes to Rajmahal he must stay there and wait till a steamer comes. The first thing he must do when he arrives there is to ask for the steamer that is there so that he may not lose the opportunity; should it not be there, when he comes, then he must wait for it and if it should be for 8 or 10 days then he can live in the Hotel [Dak bungalow?] I do not think it will cost him more than Rs. 3 a day. When he reaches there he shall send me a few lines at once and so from Karhagolah, Kishanganj, Titulayah and Punkabari to let me know how he is and how he gets on. Fred will also find by the indigo planter, Mr. Palmer, close by Karhagolah, Purnsah Post Office, and [by?] Mr. Patty and Mr. Webb and [at?] Pankabari. He must take the greatest care of his money that it is not stolen from him and a servant he must have along with him. Tell Mr. Pecise to give you one and what you think, my dear Fred, you require for your way ..... take advice of what

he says. .... now, dear Andrew, Sam is more in your charge to see that he keeps himself proper in every respect, that he is dressed proper and take care of all his clothes. You know Sam is very careless. I hope he has improved now. Keep him on and see that all his wants are supplied, that he is not to hunger or to suffer. We are all pretty well."

<u>July 10th, 1861 final letter to Calcutta.</u>
Mary Stölke's death was mentioned in the last letter. She was the daughter of Joachim, Granny's eldest brother. He married Grandfather's sister, lived at *"Steinthal."* Their children, my father's cousins, were John, Willie, Mary, Lizzie (Bessie). Mr. Sinclair, betrothed to Mary, married Bessie after her sister's death. John and Willie were at Doveton College. They too became tea planters, living all their lives on their own garden *"Rishihat."* They never married. Mary's death is described:

"Tell them [John and Willie who were in Calcutta] that they shall look up to the Lord. It is His doing and we must submit, and that what he finds good for dear Mary shall also be good for us though we may not understand it at present but we shall in heaven praise Him for His works."

Blessings from Old Letters
Frank continues:
"These original letters written in 1860/61 were kept by my father and later handed over to Granny who evidently treasured them. Some 40 years later, when she was 84, she returned them to my father on his 61st birthday with the following letter dated Sept. 29, 1902."

"Dear Andrew,
This is the anniversary of your birthday. Let me wish you many happy returns of the day and God's richest blessing for the New Year. Will you accept this handkerchief as a small token of my love, my dear? I also sent a packet of letters which Father wrote to you when you were at the Doveton College. It will cheer your heart to read them after so many years. Keep them carefully with you. They will talk to you again when you are 84 years of age. I often read old letters and they do cheer the heart. We read them all before I packed them up to send them to you.
With much love,
Your ever loving mother,
S. Wernicke."

"Granny's hope that Father would live to reread the letters when he was 84 years old was not fulfilled. He died 18 months later at the age of 62. By a curious co-incidence, I have been able to pass them over to his daughter Ethel to read them in her 84th year. Father's life at Doveton College ended at the close of the year. Letters and testimonials show the high regard in which he was held at the college. "His orderly conduct." "High principles which activated all his actions." "The importance of the influence he had on his fellow pupils." "Had every prospect of attaining high academic distinction and I therefore regret that circumstances compel him prematurely to relinquish his studies." "A modest and intelligent lad."

When Andreas Wernicke wrote in his last letter to Calcutta referring to his niece's death: *"What He finds good for dear Mary shall also be good for us though we may not understand it at present; but we shall in heaven praise Him for his works,"* he may possibly have had a premonition that his own end was near. Sophie recalls that fateful and illuminating experience:

"The cares and anxieties of those days were increased all the more as the condition of my dear husband was unfortunately getting worse day by day, until finally on the 1st of September 1861, after ten years of grave and certainly painful suffering, he was called to a better world. It was a Sunday and as soon as he was awake he felt that it was going to be his last day. So he asked me to call all his friends together and to tell his children that they were not to leave the house, in order to be nearby if he should desire to see them for the last time. I did what he wanted and then went back into the room to seek comfort in a hymn book for the coming heavy hours. There I found the verse:-

> **If I on mine own strength rely,**
> **My way from Thine would surely lead;**
> **But now take heart! I durst not fly,**
> **And in my hour of greatest need**
> **Almighty God himself shall stand**
> **With heavenly power at my right hand.**

As my eyes lifted from this text, it seemed to me as if a figure of light was standing before me which spread such radiance in the room that I had to close my eyes again. Then I sat down beside my husband's bed. He put out his hand to me and said; "I know I am a sinful man, but if God is merciful and his Word true, than I am saved; for I firmly believe this and I shall await you too in heaven." The day was drawing to its close, our friends came together and assembled by the deathbed. He stretched out his hand to us all in farewell and we stood in deep emotion and quiet prayer around his resting place. Then the golden rays of the sinking evening sun broke through the clouds and with a strange glory lit up the face of my dying husband and friend: ..... 'At even time it shall be light.' He with whom I had always found consolation and counsel throughout all the necessities of my life had now indeed been taken from me. He had now left me alone with my eight children, but now too I clung all the closer to my God and he has shown that he is 'the righteous father over all that may be his children in heaven and earth.'

Sophie was 43 years old when she lost her husband. It must have seemed like the end of her life, for on that September day her story comes to an abrupt close. She does not even mention that she had given birth to a baby-boy in June, who might have been a great consolation in her bereavement, had he not died twelve days after his father, and been buried in the same grave. Two such precious losses within a fortnight must have been hard to bear.

The next forty years Sophie puts into one paragraph. One has the feeling that she is not speaking of herself but of the lives of her children for whom she struggled and fought most heroically:

"So that we might gather together the necessary means of sustaining our livelihood, I had for some time now opened a small shop, in which I sold garments, provisions and almost anything else to the Europeans living here, and in spite of the great uncertainties of the roads, most of the goods required fortunately always reached us. Also I received a modicum from the rent of some houses, so that I could send my children to school either in Calcutta or Darjeeling. The eldest son took his qualifying examination and then helped to teach his brothers and sisters. As the sons grew up I had them instructed in the cultivation of tea. Through this they gradually made their way up so that they themselves were able later either to buy or establish large tea gardens. In the meanwhile each of them had also built their own friendly home in the beautiful surroundings of Darjeeling, and the five grandchildren and three great-grandchildren are the companions of my old age, for which I cannot thank God enough. For all the work and the endeavour, all the distress and destitution, all the tears and anguish were not in vain, but God has richly blessed it all. My life was indeed a journey passing between cares and coffins, but I have learnt the truth of the words: 'From the narrows out into the open, from the depths up to the heights the Saviour leads his people, so that they might perceive his wonders' or as the Lord has promised to his folk:-
"At even time it shall be light!"

19. Johann Wernicke in old age circa 1855

SUPREME COURT of Judicature
at Fort William in Bengal Ecclesiastical Side

In the Goods of Johann Andreas Wernicke deceased
Commission Returned and filed this 11th day of November, 1861

R. Belchambers
Duty Registrar

Probate granted to Sophie Elizabeth Wernicke the date executive this 23rd day of November, 1861

R. Belchambers
Duty Registrar

FORT WILLIAM IN BENGAL

Victoria by the Grace of God of the United Kingdom of Great Britain and Ireland Queen Defender of the Faith.

To Dr. Campbell the Superintendent, Dr. Collins the Civil Surgeon and Captain Fitzgerald Executive Engineer, all of Darjeeling GREETING.

We having good confidence in the carefulness and circumspection of you the said Dr Campbell Dr Collins Captain Fitzgerald do by these presents give you or as many other of you full power and authority to swear Sophie Elizabeth Wernicke and Joachim Stölke both of Darjeeling to the truth of their affirmations and also to administer the oath of an Executrix to the said Sophie Elizabeth Wernicke the sole Executrix named in the last Will and Testament of Johann Andreas Wernicke both of Darjeeling in the province of Bengal a German deceased the form of which oath we hereunto annexed when you or any or either of you have administered the oath aforesaid to the said Sophie Elizabeth Wernicke then you or any or either of you are to return the same to the Registry at Darjeeling of our Supreme Court of Judicature at Fort William in Bengal (p.119) under your hand and seal or the hand and seal of you or as any or either of you without delay together with the original Will herewith enclosed to you and other Commission (Title?) ***** name *****
Chief Justice at Fort William aforesaid the sixteenth day of September in the year

of our Lord one thousand eight hundred and sixty one.

Joseph Goodine (?)
Registrar

*** *Judge I O Banerjee*
Proctor

The execution of this Commission appears by a certain schedule hereunto annexed

J. C. Collins
Commissioner

The Executive Oath
Sophie Elizabeth Wernicke

You swear that you believe this to be the last Will and Testament of Johann Andreas Wernicke late of Darjeeling in the Province of Bengal a German deceased and that you are the Sole Executrix therein named and that you will faithfully execute the said Will by paying debts and legacies of the said deceased as far as his effects will extend and the law oblige you will cause all the said effects to be appropriated and make a true and perfect Inventory of these and exhibit the same to the Honourable the Supreme Court of the Judicature at Fort William in Bengal from six months from this day and that you will likewise render a true and just account of this your Executrixship and deliver the same unto the same Court on or before the fourth day of October which will be in the year of Our Lord one thousand eight hundred and sixty two.

So help you God
S/d. *S. E. Wernicke*

Sworn at Darjeeling the 11th day of October in
The year of Our Lord one thousand eight hundred and sixty one

J. C. Collins
Commissioner.

In the Supreme Court of Judicature at Fort William in Bengal Ecclesiastical Side

In the goods of Johann Andreas Wernicke, deceased

We Sophie Elizabeth Wernicke of Darjeeling in the district of Bengal sole Executrix named in the last Will and Testament of the deceased so named and Joachim Stoelke of the same place one of the subscribed wherefor thereto severally make oath and sign as follows

FIRST I Sophie Elizabeth Wernicke for myself say that Johann Andreas Wernicke my husband the deceased wherever named who was in his life time and at the time of his death a German and inhabitant of Darjeeling aforesaid departed this life on the first day of September one thousand eight hundred and sixty one at Darjeeling aforesaid having first duly made and published his last Will and Testament in duplicate bearing date the thirty first day of August one thousand eight hundred and sixty one the original and duplicate copy thereof are hereunto annexed and marked respectively with the letters A and B and appointed me the sole Executrix thereof and leaving property and effects both real and personal and leaving personal property with the local jurisdiction of the Honourable Court.

SECOND I Sophie Elizabeth Wernicke for myself further say that besides property and effects real and personal the said deceased left divers outstanding Claims and Debts due to him which cannot be collected and got in without Probate of the said Will of the said deceased and that among such outstanding claims there are some against the Government of India which Dr Campbell the Superintendant has refused to entertain without such probate.

THIRD I Joachim Stoelke for myself say that I together with Dr Vaughan and G Treutler were present and did see the said (p. 121) Johann Andreas Wernicke duly sign publish and declare on and for his last Will and 'Testament the said papers writing hereunto annexed and more respectively with the letters A and B and that the said Johann Andreas Wernicke so signed published and declared his said Will in my and the said Dr Vaughan and C Treutler presence all being present at the same time.

FOURTH I Joachim Stoelke for myself further say that the name and signature

Johann Andreas Wernicke appearing at the foot of the said papers writing A and B respectively are that of the party executing the same and the names and signatures of J Stoelke Dr Vaughan and C Treutler also appearing at the foot of the same papers writing respectively are the parties attesting the due execution there are in the respective proper handwriting of the said Johann Andreas Wernicke the deceased abovenamed are the said Joachim Treutler the said Dr Vaughan and C Treutler.

FIFTH I Joachim Stoelke for myself further say that the said Johann Andreas Wernicke at the time of making signing publishing and declaring the same Will hereunto annexed and marked was of sound mind and disposition annent memory and understanding.

Above named deponents Sophie Elizabeth Wernicke and Joachim Stoelke were severally this 4th day of October 1861 before me.

S F Wernicke

J Stoelke

J. Collins
Commissioner.

A referred to in the annexed affidavit of Sophie Elizabeth Wernicke and Joachim Stoelke severally sworn this 4th day of October 1861 Before me.

J. C. Collins
Commissioner

In the name of our Lord and Saviour Jesus Christ Amen.

I, Johann Andreas Wernicke at present of the District of Darjeeling in the Province of Bengal in the East Indies being of sound and disposing mind and memory do hereby declare this to be my last Will and Testament (p. 122)

FIRST I give and bequeath my soul into the hands of God who gave it and my body to be decently committed to the earth from whence it sprung.

SECOND I will and direct that all my just debts funeral expenses and other related charges of proving this my Will be found of my estate by my Executrix hereafter mentioned.

THIRD I will and bequeath all the rest and remainder of my property and effects whatsoever and wheresoever real and personal of whatsoever description unto my beloved wife Sophie Elizabeth Wernicke and I do hereby appoint and constitute my said wife to being the Executrix of this my last Will and Testament and of all my own and personal property whatsoever and wheresoever. I further request and desire that should my beloved wife Sophie Elizabeth Wernicke after my death be desirous to enter again into marriage that at (?) that time all my real and personal property be then divided in nine equal shares between my said wife and my eight children that is to say my wife Sophie Elizabeth Wernicke one share, my eldest son James Andrew Wernicke one share, my second son Frederick Joseph Wernicke one share, my eldest daughter Maria Wernicke one share, my third son Samuel David Wernicke one share, my second daughter Sophie Elizabeth Wernicke one share, my third daughter Emma Julia Wernicke one share, my fourth daughter Augusta Rose Wernicke one share, and my last and youngest son Wilfred Benjamin one share.

FOURTH I appoint and constitute my said wife Sophie Elizabeth Wernicke as sole guardian of all my said children and desire that they be all properly educated.

FIFTH I hereby formally revoke and make void all former Wills, Testaments and Codicils by me at any time heretofor made in witness whereof I subscribe(?) to this my last Will and Testament and also to a duplicate hereof I set my hand and seal at Darjeeling this thirty first day (p. 123) of August in the year of our Lord one thousand eight hundred and sixty one.

Given sealed delivered and declared
By the said Johann Andreas Wernicke
And for his last Will and Testament
In the presence of us who in the presence of all being present at the same at his request and in the presence of each other have subscribed our names herebelow(?)
J Stoelke
J Vaughan
G Treutler

Transcriber's Note: *The text used had been photocopied by Vivien Browne (remote cousin) at the British Library, taken back to Salt Lake City, USA for microfiche at the Brigham Young Library database of ancestry, recopied and posted to Chichester, enlarged by Chris Harris, my son in law, and finally given to me for transcription.*

*The original was probably written at some speed by an Indian court secretary, a babu, whose limited English had been shaped by training in legal jargon for his task The writing is far from the normal mid-nineteenth century English hand, and is difficult to decypher. One or two passages are therefore somewhat obscure and uncertainties are marked with (?) or ****.* Timothy Davies (Gt.Gt. Grandson).

21. A General View of Darjeeling and Mt. Kanchenjunga

CARL GOTTLOB NIEBEL

There are very few dates and facts available for the early life of Carl Gottlob Niebel before his arrival in India in 1840. After this date a fair description of the man, his work and life style can be pieced together from the reminiscences of various members of the Niebel-Wernicke Families. Some interesting information is also contained in several letters written to Mr. Start by Marina Niebel after her husband's death.

Carl Gottlob Niebel "*was born in 1810 in a village in the Riesengebirge, in Silesia (Germany) where his father was in business in tailoring in a small way. After his father's death and college in Breslau he came out to India as a missionary under the Rev. William Start of Bristol,*" wrote his only son Charles. And that covers thirty years.

How and where Start had met Niebel is a complete mystery. It must be assumed that the Gossner Mission had brought the two together and that Niebel went in the footsteps of the Wernickes and Stölkes just two years later. The "Missionary Directory" gives 1840 as "*year of arrival in India*" and Hajipur as "*field of labour*" where he found the Wernickes and Stölkes already "*labouring*".

There is no definite date for Niebel's move to Darjeeling which probably took place some time during 1843, for at the beginning of 1844 Joachim Stölke mentions that "*we meet every Wednesday morning at 10 o'clock with Br. Start and Niebel in Br. Start's chapel …*"

Niebel had been brought to Darjeeling chiefly to engage in linguistic studies and translation work – he was a university man – into the prevalent vernaculars. One of his granddaughters commented:"*Grandfather Niebel was a scholar of considerable eminence and attainment. His mastery of three local languages, Nepalese, Tibetan and Lepcha, was sufficiently advanced to enable him not only to converse in but also to write them. I have just passed on to me the original Lepcha Gospel, St Matthew, which 'he was going over with this youth making corrections.' It is beautifully and clearly printed and interleaved with blank pages. The corrections are in Lepcha, written in pencil , and are so distinct that they might have been written yesterday. Occasionally he comments in or uses a Greek word to signify more clearly the correct meaning. This "youth" refers to a young Lepcha whom Niebel 'took much trouble to instruct both in Lepcha and in English. He was going over the Lepcha Gospel with this youth making corrections. The poor boy feels his loss (Niebel's death in 1865) very much* ".

Niebel's most important translations were the book of Genesis, parts of Exodus and the Gospels of St. Matthew and St. John. On 11 Nov.1850 Carl Gottlob Niebel, son of Gottlob Benjamin Niebel, married Elizabeth Marina Lindemann ("Marina" because she was born at sea) at St. Andrew's Church, Darjeeling (She was then 22 years old and 18 years younger than her husband). At first Niebel stayed with Start at Takvar where much of his early translation work took place. On his marriage though it would appear that Start, who owned several properties at Darjeeling, gave him "Sevenoaks" where he lived until his death and *"where I (Charles Niebel) and my sisters were born."*

Several incidents are being remembered in connection with "Sevenoaks". Thus Charles:

"The Cart Road was being made during those years and once a big piece of rock was hurled by blasting on to our house. It crashed through the roof and was only stopped by boards of the ceiling while we were assembled in the room below at prayers."

One of the granddaughters has this touching story to tell:

"The house was below the Cart Road on the same side of Darjeeling as "Glöven", an unpretentious bungalow, very small for the parents and their nine children. Grandfather Carl Gottlob continued as a missionary until his death unlike the Wernickes. The salary of a missionary would have been very small and must have caused the grandparents anxious moments in order to provide sufficient food and clothing for their children. My mother (Elizabeth Bernardina) told me of an incident in her childhood at "Sevenoaks", when one afternoon she saw the postman deliver a letter to her father who was walking up and down the compound by himself. The letter contained news that his salary was to be increased by Rs.25 a month. She recalled how he stood with bent head offering a prayer of thanks that his burden had been eased. This would represent about 8 shillings a week extra to his salary. She also told me that at Christmas as children they had large paper parcels as presents. After removing endless layers of paper the present inside was an orange: also of a game played by the same children while walking back to "Holmdene" on a moonlight night. The sisters would try to step on each others shadows."

Salary was a delicate subject. Obviously, Niebel had not come to India on the Moravian plan of *"preach while you work";* Start seems to have had different plans for him right from the beginning and was responsible for his upkeep.

Considering the family with nine children, the sum provided by Start does not seem to have been over-generous. It therefore, does not come as a surprise when Rennie in his "Bhootan and the Door War" in 1865 states that:

"The London Missionary Society has so far recognised Mr. Niebel as to temporarily give him an allowance of Rs. 60 (£6) per month. With this exception his means of support are entirely derived from the rents of one or two houses in the station belonging to Mr. Start, and which of course form a precarious source of income."

After the departure of "the Moravians" in 1843, the "Tukvar Mission" was carried on co-jointly by Start and Niebel. But when Start retired to Bristol for good in 1852, *"the Rev. Mr. Niebel, the lone hard worker for a long time, continued labouring until his death on 9th October 1865."* And with his death *"the grand and admirable effort of these missionaries faded out completely."* The remark refers to the translation work into Lepcha. As for *"converting the heathen"*, the Darjeeling Handbook" of 1862 noted *"…of late Mr. Niebel has also been preaching and itinerating, but we believe one conversion has been the only manifest result."* (The "Lepcha youth" perhaps?)

Mrs. Niebel, looking after Start's property in Darjeeling, and, no doubt, still depending on his support for herself and her eight children, had a long correspondence with him of which a few extracts have been saved (the whereabouts of these and other letters, alas, cannot be traced).

<u>Parts of letters from Marina to Mr Start, a Baptist missionary, after Carl's death.</u>

"My dear Mr Start,

My last letter will have prepared you in some measure for what I have to tell you now. My dear husband fell asleep in Jesus on the 9th of this month. I feel sure you will mourn for what I and my children have lost but I sorrow not as those who have no hope. His end was very peaceful. The 23rd Psalm was very much on his mind. He often said to me when he saw me weeping 'Why should my soul a drop bemoan, who has a fountain near?' I think he hoped almost to the last that the Lord would spare him but when he felt it could not be, he quietly said 'Thy will be done'. I feel now my earthly stay has been removed, and that myself and my children are under the Lord's peculiar care and keeping, and I desire earnestly to lean on Him alone.

The Baptist missionaries have very kindly offered to take my son, who is now nearly 11 years old (Charles Niebel) into the Serampore College free of any charge except for clothes and books and I have thankfully accepted their offer. I have as you know 8 children, the youngest nearly 9 months old, and the eldest is just 14. She is a great comfort to me. When we thought her Papa was dying she came and said she wished to speak to him and then before everyone present she said 'Papa, Jesus is my Saviour and he has forgiven my sins'. You can imagine how this made me rejoice in the midst of my sorrow. I had remarked to my husband the night previous that from what I had observed in the child, I did trust that she loved the Lord. That was a wonderful comfort to him in his last hours.....

My dear husband desired me to write and tell you that during the rains which were very heavy this year (monsoon - June/Sept) he had not been able to get out very much but had occupied his time writing a Tibetan tract and in making two Nepalese tracts and he requested me to pay for the printing of the tracts out of the money which is in the Delhi Bank belonging to you. I mean the money which my brother Peter Lindeman repaid to you. You told my husband to let it remain in the bank as a reserve, in case our being in want or to use it for printing the tracts. The amount in the bank at present is about Rs:2,000. I think I shall have no difficulty in distributing the tracts as the people are very anxious to have them.

Would you also let me know about the Lepcha and Nepalese dictionaries. I suppose you have no objections to making them over to any other missionary who may be called to labour here. There is also a Tibetan vocabulary, which he was preparing. My husband never wrote much about himself or the work he was engaged in. He often told me of most interesting conversations he had with people in the bazaar and often I have heard his earnest testimony of the Lord Jesus and his solemn warning against idolatry. He often told people to pray to the Lord Jesus to have mercy on them, to forgive them their sins and give them the Holy Spirit. This he did daily as he walked along the road or passed through the Bazaar, even when he did not go out on purpose to speak to the people. He never preached, at least what is generally called preaching. But he would sit down in a shop and address perhaps only a few, but often a number of people would gather round him. It was no effort for him to speak in this way. He never seemed to tire.

There was a Lepcha youth whom he took much trouble to instruct both in Lepcha and in English. He was going over the Lepcha Gospel with this youth, making corrections. The poor boy feels his loss very much. May the seed sown in his heart bring forth fruit to the Glory of God.

We have had for the last three years a little gathering in our own house on the Lord's Day to break bread."

More Letter Extracts From Marina

To Mr Start (1)

"*Baptist churches in Calcutta sent me Rs:300 and kind friends in Darjeeling Rs.686. I have no relations in circumstances to render me any assistance and with my 8 young children I do not feel able to do anything at present towards the support of my family, but should anything present itself which I might feel able to undertake I should be very thankful to do so. My boy is still with me. I have not heard from the Serampore College. I am still occupying 'Sevenoaks.'*

I sent by last mail a letter to Mr Muller of Bristol a short account of the mission here in the hope that he might be the means of sending another here to take up the work from which my dear husband has been called away.

I should be very thankful for a few lines from you telling me what arrangements you have made with Mr Brice in case the Raja should buy the house I am living in."

To Mr. Start (2)

"*I thank you very much for your kind letter of 25th November, in which you ask about my plans for the future. I have not formed any plans, but prefer waiting for the Lord's readings, and when I can hear his voice saying 'This is the way'. I trust He will enable me to follow. I have sent my boy down to Serampore College. My other children are all girls. I am teaching the three older ones as I have always done with my husband's assistance. You ask the names and ages of the children. (14, 12, 11, 9, 6, 4, 2, 1). You mention Calcutta as affording advantages for educating my children but I should feel very reluctant to place any of my girls at school in Calcutta and it is not a place that I myself should choose as a residence.*

If the Lord should open a way for my remaining in Darjeeling I should prefer it as I have so many little ones who have been born in this climate. The Lord continues to send me help and on several occasions 1 have not known from whom the money has come. A short time ago I received Rs. 100 from the Rev. Mr Lord of the Old Church. I do not know him nor or how he came to hear of me. Mr Richards who has been Chaplain here for two years was very anxious to make an appeal to the public on behalf of myself and the children. I anticipated some such proposal might be made and requested that it should not be done, as I felt that it would be taking the matter out of God's hands, and quite opposed to the principles held by my dear husband and myself. I felt that I ought to trust in the Lord. He has helped me hitherto and I desire to cast the undivided burden of my care in Him. He giveth power to the faint and to them that have no might He increaseth strength."

She also refused help from some scientific body, probably in connection with her husband's scholarly language work on the ground that such help came from the world and without divine direction.

The monsoon had been heavy and the winter with all its unpleasantness at Darjeeling was approaching, so Marina decided to move to a warmer part of India, as her son Charles well remembered:

"After my father's death in 1865 aged 55, my mother and the family moved to Dinapore in the Plains, where my mother and your mother (writing to a nephew), then aged 15 received the rite of baptism by immersion at the hands of the Rev. Brice ..... After Christmas we all moved down to Monghyr by boat. There my mother had her first operation ..... in 1868 we all moved back to Darjeeling where my mother died in "Peace Valley" on August 19th."

22. The Grave of Johann Wernicke, Darjeeling Cemetery

As a fond granddaughter put it:

"Death released her from this burden of loving responsibility in less than three years after her husband's death."

In the Old Cemetery in Darjeeling the Niebel record reads:

Sacred to the memory of Carl Gottlob Niebel
who preached the Gospel for 23 years to the people of these hills,
and who fell asleep in Jesus 9th Oct. 1865 aged 55 years.
By his side rests his beloved child Maria Rachel aged 2 years.

Also entered into rest August 19th, 1868

Elizabeth Marina
Widow of the Rev. C.G. Niebel, aged 40 years.
"Them also who sleep in Jesus shall God bring with Him."
In Loving memory of Ada Niebel, M.D. aged 45 years, 1907

23. Darjeeling in 1850

Chapter 5

"MRS WERNIKE'S SHOP"

The financial situation of the Wernickes after they left Tukvar is somewhat puzzling. On the one hand they often seemed short of cash and depended on the daily takings of "Mrs. Wernicke's Shop;" on the other hand, there was enough to send the three boys to Calcutta for their education, which was comparatively expensive. The return trip to the school alone was a fairly costly affair. There were hints that money was in short supply, such as *"you must let me know when your money is spent, but take care at the same time how you spend it, as it is hard for us to get it,"* or *"The station is very empty this year and our sale is only a little."* Grandson, Frank Wernicke (Warwick) described how the grandparents made ends meet:

"During later years of Grandfather's life, when his activities in building and contracting must have been curtailed by progressive invalidism from gout, the grandparents may have opened some kind of general store for the sale of goods to the public to supplement the family income. The words GOODS, CROCKERY, CUSTOMERS and OUR SALE IS ONLY LITTLE appear in Grandfather's letters and would lend weight to this opinion."

Frank did not know of the existence of the Darjeeling Town Plan of 1862 on which the shop is clearly marked.

"Further evidence might also be found in the several hundred empty bottles which were used to line the borders of the flower beds at 'Glöven.' These may have been left behind by the soldiers who patronised the store and came there for drinks. CUSTOMERS could also refer to business with building materials, sale of timber and contracting."

Another source of income was the letting of bungalows to visitors. Frank writes:

"At this time ….. the East India Company were ready to make grants of land to persons who were willing and capable of helping in the development of Darjeeling as a station. Grandfather was given a plot of land in Darjeeling itself, and here he built three houses, 'Glöven,' 'Clover Cot' and 'Willow Dale.' 'Gloven' became his and Granny's home and remained the centre of Wernicke life for well over half a century, certainly as long as Granny was alive."

These houses probably partly account for the shortage of ready money, as profits were invested in their construction wisely, as it turned out. For decades accommodation at Darjeeling was lacking or dismal as "The Handbook of Darjeeling" for 1862 described:

"There is neither an Hotel or Dak Bungalow properly so-called, at Darjeeling; this is one of the crying wants of the place. There is, however, what is called a Dak Bungalow belonging to Messrs. D. Wilson & Co. This is a long narrow house divided into some five compartments, each consisting of 1 room, 1 passage or slip, and 1 bathing room. The house is not raised and is consequently wretchedly damp. The accommodation, which is inferior in quantity and quality to that of a Government Dak Bungalow, is charged for at about one half higher, whilst the cuisine is so bad and the Khansamah's charges so exorbitant, that no one ever stops there a day longer than can possibly be avoided. There are moreover minor points in which improvement is required, which we could not introduce into these pages…..," Etc., etc. For another two pages, one long wail.

Next, Capt. Hathorn in the same *"Handbook"* comes to *"HOUSES."* These are two interesting paragraphs with details which make it possible to calculate approximately the seasonal income from *"Clover Cot"* and *"Willow Dale,"* though only approximately, because the condition of the houses would determine the height of the rent.

"HOUSES. There are probably about 70 houses in Darjeeling exclusively of those belonging to the Convalescent Depot, and their rents vary from 40 to 250 Rupees a month, furnished. From 80 to 100 Rs. a month is about the average rent for the smaller ones. They are, generally speaking, single storied cottages, (or if the reader prefers, villas). As there are no two minds alike, so there are no two houses in Darjeeling alike, except where the same proprietor has occasionally produced a duplicate of his own peculiar fashion. The houses as a rule, to which there are exceptions, are not substantial or likely to last any time. They are usually made of inferior bricks, caused apparently by the clay being largely mixed with sand, an exemplification, by the way, of the old proverb, 'it is an ill wind that blows nobody good,' for this admixture of sand is a decided advantage to the tea planter.

The wood is good, but rots from constant exposure to wet. The roofs are shingled, i.e. slated so to speak, with thin slips of wood 18 by 4 inches, and tarred outside. These roofs are good, and keep out the rain very well".

He would recommend a visitor always to choose his own house, unless he has a friend at Darjeeling to select one for him. House agents never recollect any house being vacant, except one, for which it so happens, by a remarkable coincidence, they are the agents! In choosing a house, the distance from the Church and Bazaar, and whether much above or below the Mall are points worthy of consideration. The house should also be well raised, and the floors planked about 2 feet above the ground.

Houses at Darjeeling are furnished with tables, chairs, bedsteads, mattresses, sideboards, *almirahs* (cupboards), wash-handstand and basin, bathing room appurtenances, and such like. Everything else must be provided by the visitor."

What did these houses, cottages, villas or bungalows look like? Fortunately, the "Dorjeeling Guide of 1845" most helpfully provides some answers by containing two architects plans with suggestions for prospective settlers. Messrs. Martin & Co., the first and most eminent builders and contractors, no doubt, are the authors of the designs, who also worked out in great detail the list with costs of the necessary building materials. They were an old established firm of Government contractors and the leading builders at the station. They were also constantly in need of labourers, particularly specialised craftsmen in the building trade. It can be taken for granted that Andreas Wernicke did much business with them in supplying some of the most essential materials, such as wood, for many purposes.

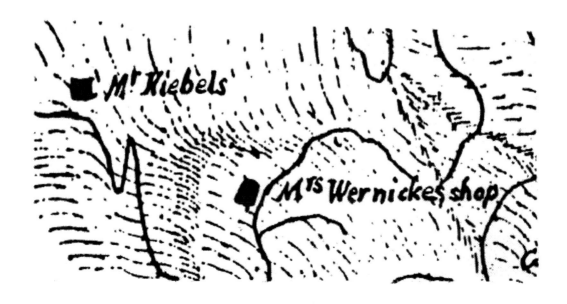

24. Mrs. Wernicke's Shop

WERNICKE AND STÖLKE HOUSES

It seems appropriate at this point to mention the *"Wernicke Houses"* as remembered by Sophie's grandson, Frank Warwick (Wernicke) with all the fond recollections connected with them. The first memorable Wernicke "residence" at Tukvar is, however, not included and most likely was never known to the third generation for, as Sophie described it, it was just a *"weakly built hut whose door was only a thin mat behind which we and our little children slept and offered no sufficient protection."* It had been provided by Mr. Start and was part of his training programme to teach *"his missionaries"* to rough it like the locals did. Fortunately this *"training"* lasted only two years, for when Start *"expelled"* them in 1843, they built their houses themselves, and this time they were *"houses,"* that is to say, solid bungalows of the type adopted as suitable for Darjeeling.

Joachim Stölke, Sophie's eldest married brother, was also given land below the Bazaar, and here he built two houses, "Peace Valley" and "Steinthal" and opened up a small tea garden of 150 acres.

"Gloven"

"Gloven" is a corruption of *"Glöwen,"* Sophie's birthplace in Germany, but became *"Gloven"* because apparently only Germans can pronounce "ö", and W = v — a gentle reminder of her "roots." Frank writes:

"Gloven" was a bungalow typical of many of the early buildings in Darjeeling. The house was built on a site made by cutting into the hillside like a step, the earth being thrown out in front to enlarge the depth of the step. This method was adopted for almost all the houses, as few level sites existed, except along the tops of the ridges. The back of the house was inclined to be dark and damp, as only a few feet separated it from the high bank. It was a bungalow of simple design and construction, raised about 3 feet from the ground to keep it dry, especially during the heavy monsoon rains. It faced more or less to the north and commanded a most extensive view with the snow-capped range of mountains of the Himalays — as dominated by Kanchenjunga, 28,000 odd feet in height, running east and west, a mighty barrier behind which lay Tibet. In the near foreground to the right, lay the greater part of Darjeeling in the arm of a horseshoe, while somewhat to the left were distant ridges covered by forests and later by tea gardens. It was in this direction that my Father and Uncle Fred made their first ventures as independent owners, opening up two gardens, Lingia and Tumsong, on adjoining ridges.

The House

In front of the house was a porch and a verandah, the latter running nearly the full length of the house. The porch was high and wide enough to permit one or even two horses to stand under cover for mounting in the rain, and to allow a "dandy" with its 3 or 4 dandy-wallahs to remain under its shelter. From the porch a couple of steps led on to the verandah. From this 3 doors led directly into (1) the drawing room in the centre, (2) on the right the dining room and (3) on the left to Granny's and her daughter Emma's bedroom. At the back and side of the house were small rooms like dressing rooms with bathrooms attached, and one of these was used as a store room for food and linen. There was no hall and access to the rooms was either directly from the verandah or from one room to the other. The roof was of corrugated iron but there were no gutters, and the rain poured straight to the ground. The kitchen and wood *godown* were to one side of the house and the servants' quarters beyond these. Sanitation did not rise to the flushing system, the work being done by a "sweeper," an untouchable.

The Garden

A description of "*Gloven*" would be incomplete without a few words about Aunt Emma's flower garden. It was quite unique. It welcomed you as you approached the house. The beds were small and of various designs - diamond, round, oblong, and they were separated by narrow intersecting paths. To maintain the soil in the beds, hundreds of beer and whisky bottles lined the beds like soldiers on parade. They were all buried with their necks well sunk into the ground, the inverted bottoms being uppermost. The flowers that remain uppermost in my mind are violets, nasturtium, agapanthus, arum lilies, fuchsias and what we called "*hen and chicken daises.*" (Note by KMD - large double daisies. My Granny grew them at Midwood and Holmdene, and I used to be given permission to make a daisy chain with them as a treat).

The End of "Gloven."

Here Granny lived for the next 63 years with her unmarried daughter Emma. After her death and Aunt Emma's, it became, I believe, a rest home for missionaries. In the great earthquake disaster of 1937, the old house perished. A photograph taken a few days after shows that the walls must just have crumbled away, the roof settling on the ruins at ground level. It was a sad sight. "*Gloven*" had been the home at various times of many of the Wernicke line for four generations, some of whom died there and some were born there. Its end seemed almost symbolic, the last chapter of the Wernickes in Darjeeling, for none of that name live there now, and the only evidence of the family association with Darjeeling and the tea gardens are the many graves bearing the name of Wernicke, Stölke, Lindeman and Niebel, and one road, Wernicke Road, named after my father.

Granny and "Gloven."

If I have written at what may appear undue length about "Gloven," it is because "Gloven" and Granny were synonymous. We all experienced in her presence great comfort, love and welcome. Her simple, unquestioning Christian faith has influenced to some extent the lives of all of us who knew her, and it gave to her strength to bear with patience and courage many heavy trials throughout her long life. Here Granny and her husband, with their children, lived the next 11 years when he died in 1861 at the age of 46. For the last years of his life he was an invalid, bearing great pain from gout and becoming increasingly feeble. I remember Grannie saying how she had him carried down to the lower and warmer slopes of the hills to a place called "Mineral Springs," where they lived in a rude matting shelter in the hope that he might benefit by taking the waters. (Note by KMD - "Mineral Springs" - *Dewai Pani* meaning "Medicine Water" - was a tea plantation on the opposite side of the Rung Dung valley from Bannockburn where my father and mother lived from 1899 till the time of my father's death in 1922).

25. Andrew Wernicke's family

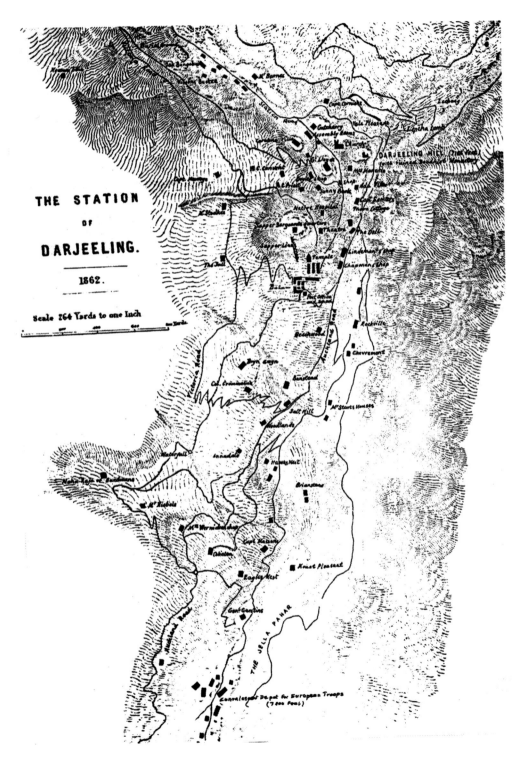

THE STATION
OF
DARJEELING.
1862.

Scale 264 Yards to one Inch

Convalescent Depot for European Troops
(7400 Feet)

THE JELLA PAHAR

EDUCATION OF THE SECOND GENERATION

The education of the surviving seven Wernicke children (out of ten) presented the parents with the problems all European parents had to face at the period and long after, until the establishment of boarding schools in the hills. There were no funds to send them abroad, and the Loreto nuns' school for girls opened in 1846, with a branch for little boys (opened in 1849), was not really a "sound" place where strict Lutheran missionaries would want to expose their children to the influence of Roman Catholic missionaries. There was also Sophie's younger brother Johann (John) who had followed his sister to Darjeeling, and who is supposed to have run a small school, though how and for whom and in what language is not clear. At any rate, he is not mentioned in connection with the education of the Wernicke children, and so the problem was solved by the simple expedient adopted by many other parents at the time — home tuition.

Sophie explained the method in her "Reminiscences": *"The eldest son took his qualifying examination and then helped to teach his brothers and sisters."* It is also most likely that Father Wernicke, who was house-bound much of the time since 1851, took his share in the educational activities.

By 1856 Wernicke finances seem to have been in a very bad shape, so that the eldest of the three boys, James Andrew, had to obtain the post of a clerk at Dr. Campbell's Cutchery at the age of 15 with a monthly remuneration of Rs. 40. This has been called "a small salary" but was really quite generous, considering that a head carpenter earned Rs. 20 and a syce Rs. 4_ per mensem , on which they had to feed their families! Obviously, those forty rupees must have made a big difference to the Wernicke budget. Owing to Sophie's tremendous efforts looking after her husband's business, running her shop and letting the two spare bungalows to visitors from Calcutta, the economic situation of the Wernickes had improved sufficiently to enable them to send the three boys to school in Calcutta. Particularly James Andrew was happy to continue his interrupted education. He left the Cutchery with a most complimentary testimonial from Dr. Campbell in his pocket:

"Now that you have quitted my office and are about to proceed to Calcutta, I have much pleasure in stating, that during the fours years that you have served under me, you have given me entire satisfaction in every way. I have had constant cause to be pleased with your careful assiduity in qualifying yourself for work and for promotion also as well as the efficient manner in which you have always discharged your duties. I wish you all success and hope you will always conduct yourself as well as you have hitherto done. - A. Campbell"

Thus the three boys set out on a cold January day of 1860 for the mild plains and Calcutta. James Andrew was now 19 years old, Fred 17 and Samuel 12. The school they were sent to was something quite special as can be gathered from a brief description in "Calcutta Old and New" of 1907. It also explains why it was chosen in preference to other "academies": there was, for instance, the prospect of gaining one or the other of many scholarships for deserving students:

DOVETON COLLEGE
(41, Free School Street)

This Institution was established on the 1st March, 1823, by John William Ricketts, "the Champion of the East Indian Community." The main objects in view were to affect an improvement in the defective system of education which then existed; and to provide for the Christian youths of Calcutta the benefit of a good education at a cheaper cost than it could then be obtained. The management was vested in a committee composed of parents and guardians and subscribers to the funds; and for years a large proportion of the Christian population owed their education to "The Parental." In 1854, a legacy of Rs. 2,30,000 was bequeathed to the Institution by Captain John Doveton, and a College Department (named after the generous legator) was added and affiliated to the Calcutta University. An Infant and Juvenile Department, and a School for Young Ladies were also formed in connection with it. The educational staff is strengthened, as necessity arises, by professors and masters from Great Britain. In addition to a number of Government scholarships annually awarded to the students of the College, who pass in the University Examinations, there is a Lawrence deSouza Scholarship for English Literature, of the value of Rs. 50 per mensem, tenable for one year, and also an Arson Scholarship of the value of Rs. 13 per mensem, also tenable for one year. The College Department likewise receives a grant-in-aid from the local Government.

The letters Andreas sent to the boys in Calcutta have already been quoted in evidence of various aspects of his character. His grandson, Frank Warwick (Wernicke), who was still fortunate enough to be able to handle and read the originals — since vanished — comments how they serve to illustrate the anxieties of parents separated from their children and the loneliness and homesickness of the boys, as well as giving glimpses into their lives. None of these letters sent by post were in envelopes. Double sheets of thin paper were used, one side being left blank for the address. The letter was folded and tucked into itself. Along with the address the word 'stamped' was written, as an extra precaution against the removal of the stamp before the postmark, date and place were added. This was a common form of pilfering especially for higher denominations. The absence of envelopes reflected the need for extreme economy which the parents had to exercise. It is curious to note that to this day paper is expensive in India and stamps are still being filched.

Andreas Wernicke died on 1st September 1861, but the boys could not attend his funeral. However, leaving Doveton College, Andrew and Sam were back to Gloven for Christmas. Andrew's career at the College had come to an end. Letters and testimonials show the high regard in which he had been held there: "His orderly conduct," "High principles — which activated all his actions," " The importance of the influence he had on his fellow pupils," "Had every prospect of attaining high academic distinction, and, I therefore regret that circumstances compel him prematurely to relinquish his studies," "A modest and intelligent lad."

The next twelve months (1862) Andrew spent at home helping his mother and determining his future and continuation of studies. He was admitted to Bishop's College and studied there during 1863 with the intention of entering the Church, but eventually abandoned the idea and returned to Darjeeling. At the end of the year 1863, Frank comments:

"Letters exist throwing some light on this period of indecision as to his career, whether for ordination or as a tea planter. It can be taken as almost certain that Andrew would never have abandoned his studies at Bishop's College, where he would have been working for a B. A. degree, unless, after his father's death, financial considerations had not required that he should find means to support his widowed mother and her family by earning his own living."

At the beginning of 1864, Andrew applied for and was given the post of Assistant on Capt. Masson's tea estate at Tukvar (Tukvar Tea Co.). When he left Bishop's College he must have given the impression that he was going to return at some time in the future to continue his studies for the Ministry, for two anxious letters followed him to Tukvar:

The first is dated Bishop's College, 29th January, 1864 and is addressed to Andrew Wernicke by the Principal, a Dr. Kay. It goes:

"Next month (23rd Feb.) I am to leave, D.V., for England. Before leaving, let me send a line to say I should like to know how you have been getting on since you left. I hope you have not wholly given up the prospect of being some time a minister of the Gospel."

And the second letter from the Rev. W. G. Cowie, Bishop's Chaplain, Bishop's Palace, Calcutta, and dated 15th April 1864, reads:

"...... *the Bishop desires me to send you a copy of his Lordship's 'Suggestions' to the Clergy, in which you will find at pp.33, 34 a list of the subjects of examination for Deacon's Orders. If you have more than sufficient time for preparing the special subjects, you should go on reading as much of the Greek Testament as you can.*"

With the benefit of hindsight, it is possible to speculate on Andrew's motives for leaving Bishop's College. One reason, no doubt, was to help his mother; but was this the only consideration or had this always serious and thoughtful young man come to doubt his vocation as a preacher of the Gospel?

For [example] the decision to give up an ecclesiastical career may also indicate the beginning of a spiritual development which led Andrew away from all organised religion and to the rejection of the Christian dogma. His notes, written down later at moments of quiet contemplation, would undoubtedly have shocked his parents. On the Crucifixion and Christ, he wrote:

"*The system that requires God to cause God to die in order to appease God, is on the face of it a priestly structure to keep men in subjugation. And so far Christian superstition is on a par with the worst superstitions that have ever existed.*"

His thoughts on the Resurrection are equally "heretic":

"*Birth, growth, full life, then decay and death. This is the order. By the repetition of that order, God keeps his world ever new. The old are removed and the new come. Individuals never reappear. The new are now living, never the old restored. Yet the world's best talent is employed on killing this patent truth and preaching the fiction of a resurrection ....*"

"*Of God I know nothing except by His working in me and around me. Bibles only contain men's thoughts of Him. God's Spirit I believe to be His influence in the world (an influence we have all felt) which has its parallel in the influence of any good man or woman, with this difference, that it is much more potent and much more present to us. We have personified that influence and made it a separate person.*"

"*God's Son is the title we give to the man, who according to our notions, best fulfilled the Great Father's will and who was full of good will to his brothers and sisters in the world — not an INCARNATION.*"

Perhaps it is all best summed up in this conclusion:

"Let our religion, our worship consist not so much in praying or kneeling as in silent, persistent obedience to the known moral and physical laws under which we live, and which we may take to express the will of the world's Author — in common language, the will of God."

Here are a few more quotations from Andrew's jottings which, though undated, clearly suggest that his spiritual development was most likely the reason for his abandoning the plan of a Church career:

A Plea for God.

The common notion that God helps us by listening to our prayers and by direct interference on our behalf may be wrong. But if He does so by an arrangement by which common sense, hard work, right relations with our fellow-men, things and circumstances, humility and an unfailing trust that these will help us out of our difficulty, He will help his children even out of great mistakes they have made, and make the bowed ones walk erect again. The recovery is as much His doing as if He had interfered directly to bring it about. At the bottom there is really no difference between the old believer and the new. The ancient ascribed the result to Him or to Providence, the modern to His arrangement of things, and so not the less to Him. The objection to the name God in much the same way falls to the ground, if we mean by it the hidden Power and Intelligence which arranges all things, it matters little by what name It is called. Perhaps the common name God or The God is better than any other we could employ.

Ideas of God

The masses will probably never rise to the conception of impersonal force as operating in the world. We cannot conceive of anything without a cause, and so we go back to a cause for everything; and that is popularly called God. But it is after all only a theory, and we have no right to form any conception of God. The Universe may have resulted that way or some other way as far as we know.

Our Ignorance of God's Nature
I don't know that we know nearly as much about God as we sometimes think we do. We know something of Him through what He has made, we know something of Him through the laws He has established, and we shall do well to study them and

live in accordance with them for we live under them and there is no escaping them. But though we may know all this, we may after all know very little about the Great Lawgiver; about Him upon whom we and all things stand. He has not revealed Himself except by His works and by his laws. What the Bible says of Him, is only what men have seen of Him through these means.

God (or Nature) and Prayer

When you begin to perceive that God (or Nature) works, not by answer to prayer, but by the operation of law, you will at the end set about getting out of a difficulty by making use of your powers of mind and body; and you will not be less thankful to Him who gave them to you, than you were before to Him, who you thought interfered on your behalf.

Beliefs of Salvation, Immortality and Forgiveness

I do not hold the forgiveness of sins because I see no evidence for it. I see only faults, followed by the punishment The Eternal has attached to them. I wish that others saw this too, for they would take better care to avoid them. For every wrong act we are undoubtedly the worse.

I do not hold the efficacy of prayer; but the importance of simple and instant obedience to what our hearts (the voice of God within us) tells us is right, and I am sure this lifts a man into the Kingdom of Righteousness, which was Christ's purpose to establish in the world.

I see no evidence for the immortality of the individual. He derives his beginning from his parents, and ends his life when his strength is exhausted. The spirit and matters of which he is formed going back into God's greatest workshop — the Earth; where, unlike our workshops no material is lost but every particle is used again — the world so being kept ever new. And for Salvation, a man must look to himself and not to another, however many may be the helps he may avail himself of on the way to "the freedom of the Spirit." We have churches to tell our young men and women of their spiritual duties and teach them benevolence, but no institution to teach them to keep close to their temporal concerns, to facts and to nature, which is far more urgent.

I had written thus far when I felt a shock, "Is that so?". Neither can be said to be "more" important, for each rests on the other and is supported by the other, and the neglect of either is followed by disastrous consequence.

Baptism and The Lord's Supper

Do let us remember that Baptism and the Lord's Supper are symbols only of purity and communion with God, and not means of grace; that improvement in life comes only of resolutely pursuing the right and the true.

The Impossibility of Miracles

Miracles are human imaginings at a time of great ignorance of physical laws and of the workings of the human mind; of how a being of benevolence and wisdom and power exceeding that of the best of the Greek and Roman gods would have dealt with human infirmities. In such a state of society, the imaginings are soon taken as facts and recorded as facts. We readily persuade ourselves of the things we think and wish to be true. Yet the good thus imagined is greatly exceeded by the good done in the world by a truer conception of the ideal man and by our endeavour to realise him in our own experience. The old ideas of what God and Christ have done for us are rapidly being replaced by truer notions of what men can do for themselves by means of the power God has given them and by the example Christ set before them.

Churches

The Church has as ever more a deep-laid and well-centred scheme for keeping up a party; while its intention is the moral elevation and education of man. It has often been discussed whether churches are human or divine institutions, but there is little doubt that they are ecclesiastical institutions, built up on the general human desire to do better and to do what is right, however great man's shortcomings may be. On the high wave of this desire the priests of all nations have ridden triumphantly; but too often they have used their leading to the confusion, and mental and spiritual bondage of their flocks, instead of helping forward their enlightenment and their emancipation from superstition, and then helping and building them up in true manhood. (In all ages there have been more false prophets than true). Only a very few have been true shepherds, and have recognised in the general desire to do better the Divine spark in the human soul, and fostered it in themselves and others to a higher life, and to a recognition and realisation of our true relation to the seen and the unseen. All honour to these noble souls! But it is very difficult for a man to shake himself free from the influence of his early training, and training of a priest is not favourable to the growth of a free spirit, and to the cultivation of truth, which is essentially free notwithstanding that it ties us down to facts."

Chapter 6

EARLY TEA PLANTATIONS

Tukvar and Mukaibari

In January 1864 Andrew, now 23 years of age, took his first step as a tea planter by joining as an assistant to Captain Masson at Tukvar Tea Estate. It was there that he had the great misfortune to meet with a gun accident. Using an old-fashioned muzzle-loader gun, he returned to his bungalow from green-pigeon shooting. The gun had been wetted by rain. Resting the gun on the edge of the bed, he was wiping it down when it slipped to the floor, exploding with the concussion, and discharged the shot which shattered the left hand and wrist. He must have suffered great pain, for it was not until the following day that arrangements could be made to carry him in a dandy to Darjeeling, where the arm was amputated below the elbow. In spite of this handicap, he used to ride everywhere, up and down on the hills on his ponies, and he also enjoyed an occasional shot with his old gun and many games of billiards, resting the cue at the elbow joint or using the billiards' rest. One of the granddaughters tells how, as a child, she was always fascinated by her Grandpa's left arm with a knitted sock over it. (In photographs, the right hand and left arm are always placed in such a way as to hide the fact of the missing left hand).

The early days of Andrew's life as a tea planter at Tukvar and Mukaibari are described in a long column of appreciation in the Darjeeling newspaper after his death in 1904:

"Mr. Wernicke started his tea planting career under the late Capt. Masson full 40 years ago and remained there as an assistant for 3 years. While at Tukvar he planted out the 4th division, which taken as a whole remains the first bit of planting done for that Company. On leaving Tukvar at the end of 1865 he took over the management of Makaibari (Kurseong & Darjeeling Co.), which, with the other Tukvar (now of the Lebong Co,), were the first Darjeeling gardens worked to a profit. Thus in 1867, he with another planter were the first to demonstrate that tea gardens in the hills could be remunerative if worked with economy and industry, thus leading the forlorn hope of tea, as it were, when such old planters as Mr. Halifax and Mr. Harold had actually withdrawn for a time in despair of success in the hills."

Carl Niebel, co-worker at the "Start Mission" and friend and neighbour of the Wernickes, had died in 1865. He left behind a sick wife, Marina, with eight children of whom the eldest was 14 years old, in very straightened circumstances. What happened next (two years later) is tenderly told in son Frank's, Family Annals:

James Andrew Wernicke = Elizabeth Bernardina Niebel

"It seems to me that this is the place to refer to my mother's marriage to Father in the last few months of Marina's life. With her mother seriously ill and to a large extent unable to care for her young family of eight, it fell to my mother to assume responsibility of looking after her brother and six sisters. One can well imagine Grandmother Marina's anxiety for the future of her children and what a relief it must have been to her when Father came through and asked for mother's hand in marriage. Father was now in a position to offer a home as he was manager of Mukaibari T E at Kurseong. I think it is questionable whether this was a love match. He was 26 years old and probably wanted someone to look after him in his home. The distressing plight of the Niebel family, for several years friends of the Wernickes, may also have prompted him to choose marriage as a means to help them. In 1918, when I came home on leave to Darjeeling at Christmas after the Armistice in the First World War, my mother spoke to me of her marriage and how on the night before the ceremony she went weeping to her mother and asked to be allowed not to marry Father. It is permissible at least to guess one of her reasons. She was only a child of 16 years and 2 months. Grandmother Marina however persuaded her to go through with the ceremony, emphasising that, as the eldest, she ought to put aside any personal feelings and consider rather her duty to the young family, whom she would be in a much better position to help by her marriage. Certainly throughout my father's life he again and again came to the help of mother's brother and sisters, when there was trouble or difficulty."

And thus it came to pass that Andrew Wernicke (aged 26), manager of Mukaibari Tea Estate, married Elizabeth Bernardina Niebel (aged 16) at the Baptist Chapel at Monghyr, in 1867.

It will appear that in those early days of tea planting, anyone with two or three years' work experience on a tea garden thought himself qualified enough to set up business for himself. In spite of initial disappointment, the general prospects seemed promising enough for someone like the Wernicke brothers to aspire to the ownership of a tea garden for themselves. They were willing to work hard and live frugally for the first four or five years after planting until the tea became marketable, and put up with what now would be called rather primitive living conditions. And so Andrew and Fred decided to launch out on their own and join the pioneers.

For some years, the Government had been anxious to develop the tea industry in the hills. For instance, in 1894 Andrew remembered in a speech at a banquet, how as a boy of fifteen, he witnessed the distribution of tea seeds in 1856:

"I recollect quite well, when 10 maunds [800 lbs.] of tea seed was got by the Government and distributed by 10 or 5 seers [1 seer = 2 lbs.] to Eurasians, Europeans and natives to make a trial of. I know where some of this seed was planted and when I see the plants grown up from this seed, I feel a pleasure in knowing that they are the oldest in Darjeeling."

26. A Path through the Jungle at Tukvar; 1868

Life at Lingia and Tumsong

It was 1864 or 1865 that the brothers availed themselves of a Government offer of land at a nominal figure to anyone of tea garden experience. The land at Lingia, comprising some 550 acres, was bought for Rs. 600. It was probably partly under native cultivation, chiefly of maize and partly jungle, and work had to begin from scratch. Actually, they cannot have been too badly off, since Andrew carried on at Mukaibari and had his manager's salary, which should have supported Fred as well (at Soom till 1872) if and when he needed help.

Frank recorded:

"The first tea was put out by an ex-sergeant round where the manager's house was finally built, Fred coming over from Ghoom to supervise the work. Working in close partnership, the two brothers would have supervised the terracing of the hillside and planting of young tea from a nursery already established, building roads and bridges, connecting the mountain streams from nearby jhoras (ravines) by channels to carry water to a large tank, from which the water was conveyed by pipes to the factory to operate the water-wheels and at a later date, the turbines. At about the same time as this development at Lingia, the neighbouring spur at Tumsong was taken over as a free gift from the Government and laid out on similar lines as a tea garden. Tumsong covered about 440 acres. Both gardens were some 12 - 15 miles from Darjeeling. The elevation varied from the top to the bottom of the garden by 2,000 to 3,000 feet. The temperature at the foot of the gardens made it possible to grow such fruit as bananas, guavas and pineapples."

In 1872 Fred left Goom to conduct and personally to control the work at Lingia. At first he lived in a small roughly built bungalow on the factory site, watching over the building of the factory and planting out the tea. Here he lived as a bachelor for several years. About 1878, when Ethel was 5 years old, Father and Mother left Mukaibari bringing Ethel and Ernest with them to join Fred at Lingia. As there would have been no room in Fred's bungalow, they made shift at first by living in the factory itself, occupying the long upstairs room, which ran the length of the factory and was used for the spreading of the newly-plucked leaf. This room was divided by light partitions into bedrooms and a bathroom, and meals were taken in one of the downstairs rooms of the factory. All water had to be carried by hand from a nearby stream, and lamps and candles provided light at night. (The tea manufacturing process lasts from March to November, so the factory would not be in use during the Winter. Hence its use as a temporary living place).

The manager's house was at last completed and they moved across to occupy it. It was now possible for Fred to bring his bride, Hannah Lindemann, our mother's cousin, to live at Lingia, the two families sharing the house. Fred's first-born, a boy, was born in November 1868 but died a few weeks later. This was a great grief to the parents. Their remaining two children, Winnifred and Gertrude, were born in 1879 and 1881. While Father was at Lingia, Bernard, Harry and Fritz (Derrick) were added to the family. About 1878/9 Father moved across to Tumsong on the neighbouring ridge. I was born at Gloven in 1881 while Father was still at Tumsong. His health, unfortunately, began to suffer and he was obliged to relinquish the management of Tumsong for a year or so and retire to Darjeeling. His return to the tea garden, however, proved too much for him, and in about 1884 he finally retired from active management to live at "Willow Dale" in Darjeeling for the next 8 or 9 years. Fred continued to live and work at Lingia long after Father had retired, but was himself obliged to retire as an invalid with rheumatism. Among my happiest childhood memories are those days spent at Lingia.

The opening of Lingia and Tumsong was a bold and arduous venture for Father and Fred, and it was only by exercising the most rigid economy and sacrificing even the simplest of luxuries that they were able to achieve their objective. It takes 5 or 6 years before the tea bush comes into bearing and manufacture can begin. These must have been lean years indeed, waiting for the first returns from the sale of their tea. Their labour and self-denial were amply rewarded later with such success as they could never have dreamt of, so that these sons of poor stranded German missionaries were able to send their own children to England and have them educated at well-known public schools (all except the eldest son, Ernest), and enable them to enjoy so many things, which their father and mother had never known or thought possible in those days of their early struggle."

Life at "Willowdale"

"I think we all look back on our life at "Willow Dale" with a peculiar sentimental attachment. It was only a small bungalow with drawing room and dining room facing the verandah. From these rooms you entered two bedrooms at the back, with dressing rooms and bathrooms attached. (KMD - bathroom meant a zinc tub, no water laid on and a commode). The accommodation was stretched to its limits to house the family. Father slept in one dressing room which he also used as an office. Ernest, Bernard and Derrick slept in one bedroom, Mother and I in the other, while the adjoining dressing room was occupied by Ethel. (Henry must have died by then - Kathleen M Davies). The congestion was relieved by the departure of Ethel and Bernard in 1887 for their education at Cheltenham, to be followed at intervals, in subsequent years, by the rest of us children. Although "Willowdale" was only a bungalow and small for the needs of the family, there was about it a sense of surrounding openness of space, with more hours of sunshine rather than with the larger and roomier houses of "Holmdene" and "Midwood" to which we finally moved. "Willowdale" was also one of the old houses built by Grandfather Wernicke, and only a few minutes walk from Granny at "Gloven." Our life there carried on in the simple, rather austere and harmonious tradition established by our missionary grandparents."

'Holmdene'

"Holmdene" was one of the larger houses recently built by my father, the other being "Midwood." At "Holmdene" we had a more spacious home and were in closer touch with the social life of the station, into which for the first time we slowly edged our way, till by degrees, it took its place normally with other interests. Here Wilfred was born in 1893 and from here Derrick and I left for England in 1894. It was not till 14 years later in 1908 that I returned to Darjeeling after entering the Indian Medical Service.

More Tea Gardens

"My father's life in Darjeeling left him little time for leisure. In partnership with his brother, Fred, they extended their interest in tea with the purchase of more tea gardens, first Pandam, the rifle range part in 1888, and later the main block, known as "Aloobari" ("Potato Garden") in 1892. When the rifle range part of Pandam was bought, Father took Derrick and me as little boys, to show us the new property and we heard the town crier announcing his purchase, as he beat his tom-tom, beginning with the words 'Biki Renni ke hokum hai' ('By order of our Lady Queen, take notice that Wernicke Sahib has etc')

On our arrival at the factory, Father was asked by some of the old factory hands to give them a sign by which they might recognise his authority of ownership of the new gardens. This Father did by breaking a branch from a tree and thus giving proof that he was master and could do what he liked with his own property. This simple procedure was enough to satisfy them."

Chapter 7

ANDREW WERNICKE

"By about 1883 Andrew, unfortunately, began to suffer from rheumatism and was obliged to retire temporarily from Tumsong to Darjeeling. An attempt to return failed and forced him in 1884 to give up active management altogether and to move permanently to 'Willow Dale' in Darjeeling. But this did not prevent him from taking an active part in the running of the tea business in general, such as acquiring in 1895 Glenburn and Bannockburn Tea Estates. This acquisition could only be done by means of a large loan, ' the repayment of which was the cause of much anxiety and sacrifice for many years afterwards, for neither of these gardens paid any profit to begin with.' In fact, the purchase was so risky that Andrew, 'to safeguard and prevent a compulsory sale of his properties deed or gifted practically the whole of them to his wife and children. They included not only the gardens already mentioned, but also considerable house property in Darjeeling."

In spite of the handicap of severe rheumatic pains, Andrew took a sustained interest in the administration of the Darjeeling Municipality and administration of justice as an honourary magistrate.

There was, for instance, the notorious case of the "Beechwood" property, Dr. Campbell's old house. It must have come up for sale, and Andrew offered the Municipality the enormous sum of Rs. 50,000 towards its purchase on condition that "this ground central location be turned into a public park for the town." For some unknown reason, the offer was declined; but the incident was raised again as late as 1908 in an article in "Bengal Past & Present" (vol. 2) by which time the affair seems to have become a local scandal. The writer describes "Beechwood" grounds as "tastefully arranged and well wooded", and tradition has it that many of the big trees and rhododendrons were planted by Sir J. D. Hooker (1849). Some local irritation was recently caused by the present owner, a German gentleman cutting down trees and in the opinion of many spoiling his property. Part of the former grounds of this house are now opened up and built over with houses large and small, including a large public ice-rink." And there is a footnote to the article: "The cutting up and building over of this central site would have been avoided had Government, or rather the Municipality, seen their way to accept the public-spirited offer of the late Mr. Andrew Wernicke, who offered 50,000 rupees towards the purchase of this property for conversion into a public park. This would have vastly improved the centre of the town, now 'hideously deformed'."

27. Tukvar Tea Estate

28. Manager's Bungalow, Tukvar Tea Estate

The name of the "German gentleman" has been given mistakenly as "Fossman" but was most likely C. Forstmann. He had lived the life of a "burrah sahib" at Darjeeling for 25 years and on his return to Germany wrote a book entitled "*Himatschal — Die Throne der Götter — 25 Jahre Im Himalaya*" ("Himachal — The Thrones of The Gods — 25 Years in the Himalaya," 1926). One gets the impression of a very thorough, well-informed gentleman, but rather conceited and arrogant, and well capable of the ruthless and monstrous activities in the "Beechwood" grounds. He makes no mention of his German compatriots, although he had been aware of them. In his chapter on "Tea Culture" he recounts:

"It has been said that in those early days a piece of land of several hundred acres could be had for the price of the stamp-fees. And so all sorts of people from all kinds of social standing gave up their old professions and became tea planters. Even missionaries let the heathen undisturbedly carry on praying to their old gods and turned to the more success-promising tea planting."

If that last remark does not give him away ….. and one cannot help suspecting there had been some collusion between Herrn Forstmann and the Municipality in this nasty case of property speculation, which produced this "gigantic piece of vandalism."

Andrew's last letter written to Frank, by then in his 4th year as a medical student at Edinburgh (it was nine years since they had seen each other!) is revealing in many ways. It also throws some light on the activities at their different tea gardens at that time:

"Darjeeling, Dec. 1st, 1903.

Dear Frank,

It is with great pleasure I had your letter to me of the 12th Nov., telling me of your deep interest in your work. How interest in our work makes it pleasant, lightens it, while want of interest makes it drudgery. To some planters, their work requiring constant labour, constant thought, is a constant inspiration. To some medical men their work is the same, a constant pleasure. I hope your work may be your pleasure and that God will bless it abundantly. I will only add that I hope you will be also a man of great simplicity and frankness; wealth is evanescent. The St. Paul's School motto was '*Monite, meliora sequamur.*' Not only when taught surely, but always. I would alter the motto and adapt it for our family one: '*Recta, veraque sequamur, caelo duce,*' 'The right, the true may we pursue, God guiding.'

The righteous man has nothing to fear, from God or man, and none so erect as he. He also takes care to keep himself straight with God. It is midnight and I am unable to sleep from pain and tomorrow is the mail day and I should not like the mail to leave without a line from me.

We had hoped that the year was going to be a very good one, quality was good and prices very good. But the large quantity of tea made brought down prices and quality and the year will not be a better one than last. Still we hope to pay off Rs. 20,000 more of the debt and to set ourselves for that extent. We did wrong to borrow money for Glenburn and Bannockburn. We thought it would go on as it had been doing, but that year it went down and will probably never recover its old position though it may give 5 to 8% on the money laid out. The boys are all working away bravely, Bruce (Glenburn), Ernest (Bannockburn), Fritz (Pandam), Charlie (Lingia) - [married Fred's daughter Gertrude], Cardew (Tumsong). It is hard work and not much return, but they are cheerful and unflagging and have at least the open air to work in. They sometimes have some fun. Bruce wrote yesterday that he had shot a deer and a murghi (jungle fowl). Ernest and Fritz often bring home something they have shot. Not many days ago Ernest got a Brahmini duck in the tea [among some tea bushes]. The thing must have come to rest weary with its flight from the Tibetan lakes to the Plains. Is it not curious that Uncle Fred, Uncle Gustav [Cowley, father of Bruce and married to Mary, Grandpa's sister] the three of us should be laid up, all men of the family as Grandmama says? But perhaps the men have most of the hard work to do and much of the exposure. Uncle Fred is very patient over his rheumatic pains and Uncle Gustav in his weakness. I wish I were as they; but this is the first long period of pain that I have had from affection (sic) of the colon. I am night and day on the rack and the doctor seems unable to do anything for me.

With love,
Your affectionate father,

A. Wernicke

PS - A very happy Christmas. This will reach you just about the time."

Alas, the new Dr. Wernicke never saw his father again, for Andrew died in January 1904 …..

After his death an appreciation was written by an old friend, which illustrated many sides of his life:

"Mr. Wernicke has given many Europeans a start in tea on those gardens (Lingia & Tumsong), evidently most laudably giving preference to the sons of old planters and other old residents. All honour is also due to his example in checking the abuse in deforesting and native cultivation on his gardens, evils that have gone far to ruin the district and discredit the tea industry and its management. Though Mr. Wernicke, through his long career, has done much in his own unobtrusive way for the tea industry, it is to be regretted that as an independent owner of private gardens, disbursing his own capital and working at his own risk, he was not brought forward more prominently in the direction of the Plantations' Association and otherwise, in preference to those merely the managers and nominees of limited companies. Considering Mr. Wernicke's calm judicial mind and public spirit, it would have been more constitutional, sounder policy and better if he had. That it has been so was in no doubt in great measure due to Mr. Wernicke's quiet retiring disposition, and having never put himself forward in volunteering, club or sporting affairs (Volunteering was similar to the Territorials in England).

In regard to liberality, Mr. Wernicke's benefactions have been too numerous to particularise. For years he was a friend of education and has been a handsome donor to St. Paul's School; concerning Church and Chapel it was non-sectarian. He also gave a most liberal contribution to the station Entertainment's Committee for building purposes some years ago. His generous offer of Rs. 50,000 to the Darjeeling Municipality on the condition that the grand central location should be secured as a public park for the town, was most praiseworthy and far-seeing. Had this offer been backed up and the proposal carried through, a gigantic piece of vandalism would have been averted and the heart of the station would have been a fairy scene of beauty instead of a hideous deformity. (I think this was developed by a man called Frossman. As a child I used to hear a lot of talk about the disastrous development - KMD). In the discharge of his duties as Chairman of District Road Cars [Roadless?] Committee and Honorary Magistrate, Mr. Wernicke bestowed much time, thought and leisure. (His son Ernest followed in his footsteps as Hon. Magistrate when he was manager at Bannockburn). It was his habit to visit old friends periodically and the more thoughtful of them could not fail to appreciate his well weighed versatile conversation. A prudent counsellor, always conciliatory, he was possessed of many qualities that the District Council can ill-afford to lose. His familiar figure and calm kindly manner will be missed by many, but most of all by his bereaved wife, aged mother and other relatives for whom much sympathy is felt."

Since the story of the Wernicke Family was compiled by Andrew's son, Frank, it is perhaps not surprising that more information exists on him than on any other member of the family. The intimate portrait Frank paints must also be quoted in full. He stresses that the appreciation given above *"would be incomplete if something were not added to it of my own recollections, those of a boy up to 12 years old, the age at which I last saw my father in India, except for a few weeks the following year 1895, when he and Mother and Wilfred, then 2 years old, came to England to visit Bernard, Fritz (Derrick) and me for a holiday. (The only visit Grandpa paid to England). He took us all to spend a very happy holiday at Grasmere in the English Lake District, where we were joined by our cousins Wilfred and Gertrude. Our stay at Grasmere was enlivened one day when Kaiser Wilhelm II drove past our home in company of Lord Lonsdale. He was Kaiser "Bill" of WW1 who abdicated in 1918.*

I remember Father as a tall, slim middle-aged man, over 6 ft. in height and with a greying beard. He walked with a slight stoop and one shoulder slightly depressed, owing to the loss of his left arm. In expression his face was rather pale, somewhat care-worn and rather meditative. He seldom smiled, and I don't think I ever heard him laugh. His dress was always simple, and to my childish critical eyes, shabby. He set little store on personal appearance, maintaining that it was the person wearing the clothes and not the clothes that mattered. He always required some assistance in dressing and at meals. Mother cut his meat for him at table and we boys were constantly called upon to tie his shoelaces, actions which he found impossible to perform with only one hand. Although I never remember him ill, he was never robust and suffered much from headaches and indigestion. He felt the cold keenly and I can recall him sitting at his desk in the Winter with a shawl over his knees and a Balaclava cap on his head, working and writing before breakfast while the family was still in bed. He was a light sleeper and was usually awake long before the rest of the household, and would often spend the time before dressing, reading a book in bed, underlining certain passages or annotating in the margin. (KMD - I can remember my grandfather with a shawl on his knees, a shepherd's plaid, and sitting on his lap, and his showing me a book on Botany. He was at the end of his life and I have a picture of a tall man with a stoop and a beard. Many years later I realised that Wilfred, at about the same age, brought back to me the memories of his father.)

He set a very high moral standard for himself and his children who did not find it easy to live up to his standards. He insisted on the value of hard work, simplicity of life and education, devoting much of his time to instructing us in those subjects that were outside the school curriculum. His intention was, no doubt, praiseworthy and ultimately may have benefited us, but at the time it engendered a feeling of resentment and revolt. In the mornings, while it was still dark, about 6 a.m., he would waken us and light the lamp by our bedsides and expect us to study for half-an-hour from Greek, German of French grammars. The following half-hour would be spent on hearing the Lesson. We would then dress and ride off to School (St. Paul's - KMD). On our return from school, he would summon us during our playtime, for another period of instruction, usually in writing and English spelling. A most unfortunate result of his well-meaning efforts was to estrange and cause me to look to him in the light of a strict and stern schoolmaster, whom we, or at any rate I, resented and feared him instead of respecting and caring for him as a father. This reaction on our part probably increased a justifiable irritation towards a bunch of somewhat unruly boys. He frowned on the usual levity and fooling round of growing boys, and his quick temper sometimes overcame his self-control, when inattention at lessons or impudence would be rewarded by a smart smack on the head. (KMD - When about 4 years old at "Midwood," I was smacked by Grandpa for making a great fuss because the ayah had taken my doll's flannel petticoat as a flannel to wash my brother Ted, then known as Eddie.)

I would not, however, be doing father justice if I did not mention how every now and then, especially in the winter holidays, he allowed his suppressed concern and affection for us boys to find expression in giving us a wonderful holiday. We would set out on an expedition for about a fortnight on horseback, taking our guns with us and riding some 15 to 18 miles each day from stage to stage, with coolies to carry our luggage and servants to look after and cook for us, and resting at the end of the day in "dak" bungalows or "rest houses." Our journey would take us through tea gardens where the managers would entertain us, along the banks of the Teesta and other rivers, through forests, till we finally reached the Plains and lived in a Forest Department bungalow for a few days, taking the shooting of doves, parrots and occasional jungle fowl or pheasant most seriously as only youngsters, under 15, can. At such times, Father was all we could have wished as a friend and companion, and it is as such that I would remember him. He was also a great lover of nature. We boys were always encouraged to observe the wild-life of the jungles, to recognise the different trees of the forest, the wild flowers and orchids, the birds, beetles and butterflies. He would often call us to watch the wonderful views and sunsets on the snows and so awaken in us a love of what is grand and beautiful in nature.

If I have failed to do justice to my father's character, I can only plead that those were the reactions of a child some 60- years ago, and that my maturer judgment as a man and a father recognises his remarkable and splendid qualities of integrity and self-sacrifice for his children."

29. Andrew Wernicke

30. Andrew Wernicke and his family

FRED

The chronology of the brothers' movements is difficult to establish as the dates given in Frank's family chronicle contradict those given in Thackers Directory. The "Directory," however, is not always reliable, and data incomplete. It had been started in 1863 and only gradually became more and more comprehensive and dependable. For instance, for years after Andreas' death it gives his name as a resident of Darjeeling, meaning, no doubt, Mrs. A. Wernicke. Also the listing of tea gardens (and their spellings) is irregular. But a compromise seems possible when one remembers that one manager could frequently be made responsible for as many as four separate tea gardens. As Fred disappears only in 1873 from Soom in the "Directory," and Andrew is missing in 1877, both seem to have left at the end of the previous year, but had been working for their respective tea companies whilst at the same time looking after their own properties. This would explain how the two families and their mother and sisters survived for years without an income from their own tea gardens: Andrew and Fred were both drawing salaries sufficient to keep them all going; and Sam too was earning and doubtlessly making his contribution to the family funds. The whole Wernicke establishment appears as one happy family combine built on mutual trust, deep affection and immensely hard work.

Fred's career in the tea industry of Darjeeling can now be more or less accurately recorded: He began as assistant to Capt. Jerdon at Soom Tea Estate in 1863 and worked there full-time till 1865. When Frank wrote "In 1865 Fred left Soom to conduct and personally control the work at Lingia," it really meant that from that date on he continued at Soom on part-time terms, and at the same time was able to give his full attention to the development of Lingia, where he had at least one European assistant (who had to be paid!).

At first Fred lived in a small roughly built bungalow on the factory site, watching over the building of the factory and planting out the tea. At some time in 1867 the manager's house was completed and he moved across to occupy it. It was now possible for him to bring his bride, Hannah Lindeman, to live at Lingia. Fred's first-born, a boy, was born in November 1868 but died a few weeks later. This was a great grief to the parents. Winifred and Gertrude, were born in 1879 and 1881.

From all accounts, it can be gathered that Fred never left Lingia again and did any work that fell to his share in the running of the other tea gardens, such as Pandam (1888), Allobari (1892) Glenburn and Bannockburn (1895), from "Orchid Lea" at Lingia. He continued to live there long after Andrew had retired to

Darjeeling (1888), but was himself obliged to retire as an invalid with rheumatism.

One of Fred's nieces remembers with great affection:

"Uncle Fred I knew always in a long chair on the landing upstairs at his house "Orchid Lea" with a tartan rug over his knees. I always wondered why he was chewing and learnt years after that he chewed tobacco ….. Among my happiest childhood memories are those days I spent at Lingia."

Frederick Joseph Wernicke (to give him his full name) died in 1911, one of the valiant pioneers in the development of Darjeeling and its tea industry and the first of the Wernickes *"in tea"*.

SAMUEL DAVID

It will be remembered that Samuel David, the youngest of the three Wernicke brothers, had returned to Darjeeling from Calcutta at the end of 1861, together with Andrew and Fred. After that date, he could no longer be traced in the family records until his death in 1876. Thackers Bengal Register, however, revealed it all — or almost all. Apparently, between 1861 and 1864 — from from the age of 12 until 15 — he spent at home helping his mother and continuing his studies under his brothers guidance who lived close enough to keep an eye on his progress. Then, in 1865, he joined brother Andrew at the Tukvar Tea Estate and became the third tea planter in the Wernike family. According to Thackers Directory, he stayed there until 1870 - becoming in between "S. Ebernicke" in the Directory - and transferred to Soom where brother Fred was Assistant Manager. For the next two years the two brothers worked together whilst Fred looked after Lingia as well. 1872 seems to have been Fred's last year at Soom, and 1873 finds him full-time at Lingia whilst Sam had already moved during the previous year to Singell Tea Co. at Singell Spur.

There are gaps in Thackers Directory with regard to the list of tea gardens and their managers, but it looks as if Sam worked at Singell Spur from 1873 until illness removed him at the end of 1875. But happily, he could still enjoy the day when the three brothers became the official joint owners of Lingia, and he could proudly read in Thackers Directory: ***Lingui (meaning Lingia) Tea Estate:***

Proprietors: *J. A. Wernicke*
                 F. J. Wernicke
                 S. Wernicke
                 G.A.G. Cowley.

Sam was only 28 years old when he died from an unknown cause. His tomb is still in a reasonable condition and a not yet vandalised inscription hints at what Sophie must have felt, on that sad April day in 1876.

31. Sophie, Bernard and Ernest

DARJEELING'S RESPLENDENT TRANSCENDENCY

Queen of Hills! Darjeeling glows,
Fronting the eternal snows!
Prodigal of health, she stands,
Healing tends with lavish hands:
Convalescence gives the weak
Tints with bloom the pallid cheek,
Panacea for ills of all: -
Sanitarium of Bengal.

Heights around show scurrying streams,
Flashing silvery ribbon-gleams,
Hills with sheen, like amethysts,
Valleys deep where sink the mists.
See adown on rivers face,
Cloud-land kiss its sleeping place;
Light at morn each downy head,
Rising tensile, streaming, spread.

Nature's throne divine is seen,
Primal forest, mountain screen.
Point and range that greet the sight,
Flood the soul with rapt delight;
Spirits quickened by the scene,
Thrill with ecstasy serene.
Here, in Nature's genial nest,
Gazing, praising, blissful rest.

With the mountains' bracing air,
City taints may not compare;
Nor mafusile, deadly dull,
Where the brain shrinks in its skull;
Here, desire for food grows keen,
Gormandising may be seen;
No dyspepsia interferes,
Constitutions brave the years.

Witness, hale John White! and she,
Aged Mrs. Wernicke!
Also Sinclairs of Steinthal,
Heaven's choice blessing crown them all;
And the Webb's grand family,
Proud of its fine density! -
Mrs. Hannah, senses clear,
Christian true, whom all revere;

Mother of four splendid men,
When shall we see such again?
Handsome, tall, feet twenty-four!
Youngest, Barrister-at-Law! -
Mr. Claud Bald of Tukvar,
Healthy, trusty, popular,
Noted Planter, faithful, sealed,
Worker in the Master's field!

Wathen, Ager, Nash, these three,
Planters of integrity,
Stolke brothers, Jukes as well,
This grand trio richly swell;
Andrews, Baker, Gordon, Hasell,
Shannon, Lister, Judge and Ansell,
Weston, Wearing, Wernicke,
O'Donoghues, and Dominy;

Crossman, Cruikshank, Clark and Shaw,
Monypenny, Whitamore,
Malins, Mytten, Mackie, Brown,
Filed and Davys lower down;
Lennox, Davenport and Webb,
Irwin, - here the list must ebb; -
Years on years have felt no ill,
Staunch and energetic still.

From: Capt. J.A. Keeble, *Darjeeling Ditties and other Poems* - A Souvenir - The Homestead, Happy Valley Tea Estate, Darjeeling, 1908.

SOPHIE ELIZABETH WERNICKE (NEE STÖLKE)

Born at Glowen 7th August 1818
Died at Darjeeling 3rd August 1913

An era had come to an end in the Wernicke family history when Kathleen Wernicke wrote to her children in England from Bannockburn Tea Estate near Lebong on 6th August 1913

32. Sophie Wernicke with Emma Julia and Doris Elizabeth; circa 1910.

" *I have a very sad piece of news to give you children this mail. Dear Grandmama was taken ill, very ill, on Friday night and passed away peacefully on Sunday at mid day. Poor dear, she had often said her journey had been a very long one and she was getting very tired, so many of her loved ones had gone on before. She looked, on Sunday evening when I went over to see her, for the last time, as if she had found "Peace, perfect peace". Her face was just too beautiful for words. the years had rolled off her and she looked wonderfully young. She was just four days off her birthday for 95....".*

She had lovingly looked after an ailing husband and run a business ("Mrs. Wernicke's Shop") to support the family; she gave birth to ten children and brought up eight; and she was the centre of the Wernicke Family, providing warmth and happiness to all comers; and she became the mother of the *"Wernicke Tea Empire"* - a record of loyalty, determination, endurance, courage and profound faith in her religious belief - all much to be admired.

THE THIRD GENERATION

Education

In 1864 St. Paul's School was transferred from Calcutta to Darjeeling to the estate belonging to Bryan Hodgson, whose house *"Bryanstone"* became the new school. From the beginning the school had a hard struggle for existence. Numbers were small and the first Rectors were rather unsatisfactory. In 1877 the school had some 50 pupils and a Rector, whose interests lay more in the tea gardens he owned than in the education of his charges. A Dr. Cox, who arrived at this time to take up the post of teacher, recorded that *"the whole tone of St. Paul's was objectionable; the educational standard was beneath contempt, and the boys' sole idea of enjoyment was to cause as much trouble as they could."* The change from the old free-and-easy methods was at first much resented by the boys, who gave vent to their dissatisfaction in a riot but which was easily suppressed, the leaders being expelled. The new masters worked hard, and at the end of the year the *"Darjeeling News"* commented on the great improvement in the School, especially to the appearance and behaviour of the boys.

It will be remembered that the second generation of Wernickes (Andrew, Fred and Sam) had to be sent to Calcutta for their education at great expense and inconvenience. By the time the third generation was ready for their schooling, St. Paul's had been opened and partly solved this problem. The first to join the school, probably as a boarder, was Harry — at the age of six (?) — who attended during the reign of misrule and died there in 1874; it is not unlikely that his death was due to lack of care and general negligence. However, change in school management in 1877 and speedy improvement of standards encouraged Andrew to send four more boys (Ernest, Bernard, Derrick and Frank) also to St. Paul's, and only Wilfred went, for some unknown reason, to St. Joseph's College. In fact, Andrew became a loyal and generous supporter of the School in years to come.

Andrew had lived all his life in India and had grown up in a completely *"Anglo-Indian"* environment, and therefore acted as all Anglo-Indians at the period did when it came to the question of sound education; he sent his children to England, a college in Cheltenham.

The first batch went in 1887 (Ethel, Ernest and Bernard); the second batch followed in 1894 (Derrick and Frank). As Ernest wanted to enter the army, he was sent to a special school at Gravesend for a year; however, he failed the army entrance examination and returned to Darjeeling to make *"Tea"* his career.

33. Bernard, Derrick and Ernest

34. Kitty Davies, with Timothy, Gr. & Gr. Gr. Wernicke

Chapter 8

THE TEA INDUSTRY AT DARJEELING

In order to understand fully the role the Wernickes played in the development of the tea plantations of Darjeeling, it would be useful to trace their history to their beginnings. As no comprehensive account of it has ever been written on this subject, we can do no better than refer to O'Mally's Darjeeling Gazetteer of 1907 and his chapter on "The Tea Industry":

"The establishment of the tea industry in Darjeeling is due to the enterprise of Dr. Campbell, who was appointed Superintendent of Darjeeling at a time when attention was being attracted to the possibility of starting and developing the cultivation and manufacture of tea in the territories under the East India Company. In 1834 the Governor-General, Lord William Bentinck, had appointed a committee 'for the purpose of submitting a plan for the introduction of tea culture into India.' This committee was apparently ignorant of the fact that in 1821 Major Bruce, and in 1824 Mr. Scott, had discovered the tea plant growing wild in Assam; and much expense and considerable delay were consequently incurred in bringing plants and seed from China, and importing Chinamen to teach the people of India how to grow the plant and manufacture tea. Satisfied that a great future might lie before the industry, Government itself undertook the formation of experimental plantations in Upper Assam and the districts of Kumaon and Garhwal; in 1839 private speculation took the field, and the Assam Tea Company was formed.

In 1839 Dr. Campbell was transferred from Katmandu to Darjeeling, and there started the experimental growth of tea. The first trial of the tea plant was made in 1841 with a few seeds grown in Kumaon from China stock. It was soon found that the plant throve readily at this altitude, and others began to follow Dr. Campbell's example, seed being distributed to cultivate the plant. Writing in 1852, Mr. Jackson says in his Report on Darjeeling — I have seen several plantations in various stages of advancement, both of the Assam and China plant, and I have found the plants healthy and vigorous, showing that the soil is well adapted for the cultivation. In the garden of the Superintendent, Dr. Campbell, in Darjeeling, in the more extensive plantations of Dr. Withercombe, the Civil Surgeon, and Major Crommelin, of the Engineers, in a lower valley called Lebong, the same satisfactory result has been obtained; the leaves, the blossom and the seeds are full and healthy ….."

A year later, in 1853, Dr. Campbell, writing to the Board of Revenue in Calcutta on his attempts to establish the cultivation of the tea plant, records that: *"there are, I believe, upwards of 2000 plants now growing on different elevations, from 7000 to 2000 feet, and of different ages, from twelve years to seedlings of a few months."*

He goes on to say:

"These plantations appear to have been merely experimental plots, but by the year 1856 the industry began to be developed on an extensive scale, especially on the lower slopes, as it was believed that the elevation of Darjeeling was too high for the plant to be very productive. According to the account of a contemporary writer, tea plants had been sown and raised by the end of that year at Tukvar to the north by Captain Masson, at Kurseong by Mr. Smith, at the Canning and Hope Town plantations by the Companies attached to those locations, by Mr. Martin on the Kurseong flats, and by Captain Samler, the Agent of the Darjeeling Tea Concern, between Kurseong and Pankhabari. At the same time, Government endeavoured to supplement the efforts of these pioneers of the industry by distributing several maunds of tea-seed among the native cultivators "

"The year 1856 may, accordingly, be taken as the date at which the industry was established as a commercial enterprise. In that year the Alubari tea garden was opened by the Kurseong and Darjeeling Tea Company (which Andrew joined in December 1865), and another on the Lebong spur by the Darjeeling Mortgage Bank; in 1859 and 1864 four gardens, Ging, Ambutia, Takdah and Phubsering were established by the Darjeeling Tea Company, and the gardens at Tukvar and Badamtam by the Lebong Tea Company. Other gardens which were started at this early period were those now known as Mukaibari, Pandam and Steinthal tea
estates ...." (O'Malley)

The number of tea gardens grew rapidly, and by 1895 when the Wernickes acquired Glenburn and Bannockburn, there were 186 tea gardens in the Darjeeling area, with 48,692 acres under cultivation, producing 11,714,551 lbs. of tea! Of these the Wernickes controlled seven gardens with approximately 1,700 acres and a harvest of approximately 410,000 lbs. of tea!

GOOMBA TEA ESTATE
P.O. Chong Tong Railway station Ghoom, Acreage 86. Proprietor: F.J. Wernicke.

LINGIA TEA ESTATE
P.O. Chong Tong, Acreage 400. Proprietors: J.A. Wernicke, F.J. Wernicke, P.A. Cowley, Manager: F.A. Bruce Cowley; Assts. E.C.O. Graham and Fritz P. Wernicke

MARYBONG TEA ESTATE
Railway station Ghoom, Garden Marybong and Goomba. Acreage 170. Proprietors: P.A.G. Cowley and F.J. Wernicke.

PANDAM TEA ESTATE
Gardens Pandam, Alubari North and Alubari South. Acreage 350. Proprietors: J.A. Wernicke and F.J. Wernicke.

RISHEEHOT TEA ESTATE
(Siring) Acreage 250. Proprietors: J. Stölke, J.W. Stölke and W. Sinclair. Manager partner J.W. Stölke.

STEINTHAL TEA ESTATE
Acreage 40. Proprietors: J. Stölke, J.W. Stölke and Mrs. Sinclair (Mrs. W.)

TUMSONG TEA ESTATE
Acreage 300. Proprietors: A. Wernicke, Manager E.A. Wernicke.

ANDREW AND TUMSONG

The first time "Thackers Directory" takes a brief notice of Tumsong is in the 1876 edition: "Tumsong — propr. J.A. Wernicke — mangr. J.A. Wernicke". In 1879, the acreage has also been ascertained: "Tamsong — Acreage 250. Propr. J.W. Wernicke. Mangr. H.L. Croseman". In 1881-2 Andrew is on his own again, but by 1883 the acreage has grown to 275 and an assistant has been engaged, who stayed till 1885. The need for help, however, arose from the fact that Andrew suffered from severe rheumatic trouble and had to retire temporarily, leaving the running of the garden to C. Whitamore, obviously a good man who worked for the Wernickes at Tumsong, and later at Lingia until the end of 1887.

In 1884, Tamsong moves from the top of the "T's" (Ta .....) in Thackers Directory to the bottom (Tu .....) and becomes TUMSONG TEA ESTATE for ever after, and its acreage has further increased to 325.

It is in 1884 that Andrew is forced to retire from active management at Tumsong, but remains, nominally, the manager.

In 1886 and 1887, T.H. Blower fills a gap, but hands over, in 1888 to H.G. Coombe who, with C. Whitamore (from 1890), runs the estate until 1892 and carries on as assistant to a new manager (W. Hasell). 1893 finds the same manager with help from the Stölke side — S.D. Sinclair, who continues by himself through 1894.

All these frequent changes cannot have been very good for the estate, and the arrival of the third generation of Wernickes can only have been beneficial all round: Manager — Ernest A. Wernicke — for the next five years (1895).

By 1901, Ernest had moved to Bannockburn, and the management of Tumsong was taken over by C. C. Onslow-Graham and run with a variety of assistants until 1909.

1910 is the memorable year in which Ernest becomes proprietor with a new manager and assistant. Acreage grows to 355. Although a more permanent manager was found in P.A. McNought in 1912 (until 1917), the constant change of assistants, or even absence of assistants, must have been very unhelpful..

There is no evidence for what happened next. It must be assumed that the formation of the Lingia Tea Estate into the Lingia Tea Co. Ltd., in 1919 included the disposal of Tumsong (perhaps with a deep sigh of relief). As the Directory volume for 1920 is missing, we have to turn to 1921, where we learn that T.A. Baldry, the last manager of the Tumsong Tea Estate has become for first manager of the TUMSONG TEA CO. LTD.

A puzzling phenomenon in all the tea gardens is the comparatively frequent changeover in assistants, less so in the managers. No figures relating to remuneration are available, but it can be taken for granted that the mostly inexperienced young men were not paid very gratifying salaries, considering the exhausting efforts they were expected to put into the work. Another cause could have been the very nature of the work itself, demanding sixteen hours daily attention to the many complex processes in tea production under often difficult climatic conditions. The job must have been just too much for many prospective tea planters, who after a year or two of trying, abandoned the career.

There is an excellent description of life on the tea garden by (Sir) Edmund Cox in his account of "My Thirty Years in India". After Marlborough and Cambridge, aged about 21, he conceived the notion that going "into tea" might give him a prosperous future. Thus, he went straight to Darjeeling in 1877 where he was the guest of the Rector of St. Paul's School. The Rector also ran a tea garden as a sideline and was very much in need of teachers, and so tried to dissuade young Cox by telling him that he would be very unwise to tie himself down to any particular tea garden until he knew more of the country. Meanwhile, he recommended to him to accept the vacant post of classical master in the school on a salary of Rs. 120 a month, with furnished rooms and the food at the boys' table. But Cox remembered:

"I was rather anxious to get to the tea business as soon as possible, so I thanked him for the offer and begged for a little time to consider it. He agreed, and I went on short visits to several tea-planters. All of these were most kind and hospitable, and showed me their gardens and tea-curing sheds, and so on, and told me all about the work. The long and short of it was that I was entirely disillusioned on every point except one, and that was the magnificence of the scenery. But even here was a crumpled rose-leaf, or, considering the local surrounds, a tea-leaf; for I was credibly informed that owing to rain and cloud and fog, weeks, not to say months, might pass at a time without a view of the snowy range being obtainable. This I found by experience to be absolutely true. Of all the detestable climates that I have ever struck, Darjeeling fairly takes the cake. It can boast a hundred and twenty inches of rain a year, and the chota and the burra bursat, or the former and the latter rains, seem to cover between them ten months out of the twelve. Of course, for anyone jaded and worn out by severe work in the heat of the plains, it is a refreshing change to go up to the hills and take pleasure in contemplating a reasonably low thermometer, in spite of the rain and gloom, and the clouds that penetrate the bungalows; and children can be reared here who might die in

Calcutta. But the worst summer in England is more enjoyable than the chilly vapour-bath of Darjeeling.

You can imagine the life led by the tea-planters for months of the year in such a climate. They go out early in the morning, and stand for perhaps four hours in the ceaseless rain, superintending the work of swarms of coolies, who are engaged in pruning the bushes, picking the leaf, or weeding the plantations. Drenched to the skin, in spite of all precautions, they come in for a midday meal and change of clothes, and then go out again for the same work till the evening. Or they may, as a variety, spend their time in the sheds, where the tea is dried and cured. This part of the business is perhaps worse, for the fumes of the leaves while undergoing the process are almost overpowering, and after a few minutes only of watching the fermenting, if that is the right word, I was glad to beat a hasty retreat and seek a breath of fresh air. Then, kind as were the planters whom I visited, their mode of life seemed extraordinarily uncomfortable, unless to have a large number of incompetent servants, and a table loaded with an excessive quantity of abominably cooked meat, together with beds that made you ache to sleep in them, and pillows that might have been stuffed with stones, constituted their idea of luxury.

These details might, I suppose, have been remedied, but what was worse, and what could not be remedied, was that the price of tea was steadily going down. Some planters of an optimistic turn of mind hoped for better days, but the better days have not come yet. Further, you could make nothing out of tea beyond a bare subsistence if you slaved at it for years and years, unless you were prepared to put money, and a considerable deal of money at that, into it. It took me a little time to digest all these facts, and then it dawned upon me that I had made a considerable fool of myself in coming out to the Darjeeling tea-gardens. The question naturally arose, what to do? I settled the matter for the immediate present by accepting the offer of the classical mastership at St. Paul's School. I suppose it was about the end of January that I came to this conclusion."

He struggled with a bunch of rather unruly boys until October, when he received a letter from the Director of Public Instruction, offering him the post of Second Master at the Nizamut College at Murshidabad, which he accepted with alacrity. He never looked at tea again — except in his cup, of course .....

35. Sophie. Wernicke (Stölke), Bernardina Wernicke (Niebel),& Kathleen Wernicke (Lowis) with Kathleen/Kitty.

36. Bernardina Wernicke.(Niebel) with her sons Bernard, Fritz/Derrick, Ernest, & Frank

37. The Wernicke Family at Darjeeling Ernest, Frank, Bernard, Fritz/Derrick & "Fly" the dog.

38. Kathleen Davies (Bellew), Kathleen Davies (Wernicke), Timothy Davies, Christine Davies, KathleenWernicke (Lowis) with Alison & Suzanne.

FRED AND LINGIA

Having been started in 1865 or 1866, Lingia took almost ten years to be taken notice of, or considered worthy, to enter the list of tea gardens in Thackers Directory for the first time in 1874. Even then the mention was rather brief: "Lingay, Messrs. Wernicke & Co. Manager, F. Wernicke." (Lingay was probably the Lepcha name for the locality).

In 1875, Thackers became more detailed: "*Lingui Tea Estate. Proprs. J.A., F.J., S.D. Wernicke & P.A.G. Cowley. Manags. J.A. & F.J. Wernicke. Asst. R.H. Lindeman. Calcutta agents, Williamson, Magor & Co.*" (S.D. Wernicke had died in 1876, and had, therefore, been taken off the list. R.H. Lindeman may have been a brother of Hannah, Fred's wife). An increase of acreage to 350 is the only change in the general set-up until 1885, when R.H. Lindeman, after six years' assistance, leaves Lingia and is only replaced in 1886 by C.W. Whitamore, who had been brought over from Tumsong where he had worked for three years, and to which he returned for another three years (1890 - 1892).

In 1889 or 1890, (the volume for 1889 is missing), Ernest begins his career "*in tea*" and becomes assistant under the guidance of a more experienced other assistant, (E.J.L. Symonds), and Uncle Fred as "*superintending manager.*" Originally, Ernest had intended to enter the army and had been sent to a kind of "*crammer*" school at Gravesend for a year in 1887 (?), but, alas, he failed the army entrance examination and returned to Darjeeling in 1888 or 1889, and without further ado, took up tea planting at the age of 19 or 20. (What he did not achieve, his son Andrew Edmund did, rising to the rank of Lieutenant Colonel, fulfilling his father's ambition!).

In the following year (1891) he was already trusted as the only assistant. He most likely lived with his uncle, so that any problems arising in the course of a day could be solved instantly with Uncle Fred's help.

Lingia seems to have been the training ground for other members of the family: In 1902 Fred's nephew, Bruce Cowley, son of sister Mary, enters as assistant and advanced to manager in 1897-98. In 1895, young Stanley D. Sinclair, grandson of Joachim Stölke of Steinthal, arrived for a year; and in 1898, younger brother Fritz/Derrick is introduced into the secrets of tea production by cousin

Bruce Cowley until 1900, together with another assistant, Charlie Onslow-Graham, husband of Gertrude Wernicke, Fred's daughter.

In 1911 Fred dies, and Bruce Cowley steps in for a year until the new manager, E.C. Onslow Graham, takes over and runs the garden with one assistant and no further changes take place until the momentous date of 1919 and the *"great amalgamation"*.

Although the new name of LINGIA TEA COMPANY LIMITED appears for the first time in Thackers Directory in 1919, details of the new set-up are only available in the volume for 1921:

"Lingia Tea Co. Ltd. (incorporated in India). Capital — Rs. 7,00,000 divided in 7000 shares of Rs. 100 each. Directors — E.C. Onslow-Graham, F. Page Wernicke & A.D. Gordon. Secs. Williamson, Magor & Co., 4, Mangoe Lane, Calcutta; Post & Tel. Office, Darjeeling, Ry. Stn. Ghoom. Gardens: Glenburn & Simbong. Acreage under cultivation — Glenburn 491.93; Simbong 126.44. Total 618.37. Total gross acreage: Glenburn 1,133.92; Simbong 713.51. Total 2047.43. Elevation 3000. Mangrs. Glenburn: P.A. MacNought; Lingia E.C. Onslow-Graham; Pandam F. Page Wernicke."

ERNEST AND BANNOCKBURN

According to family tradition, the tea gardens of Bannockburn and Glenburn were acquired in 1895 with the aid of a large loan. But Thackers Directory knows nothing of the negotiations or their completion for some years. In 1895, and until 1899, it notes: "Bannockburn Tea Co. Ltd. Post Office Darjeeling. Gardens: Bannockburn (Ahlee Bong) and Minchu. Acreage, 375. Proprs. Bannockburn Tea Co. Ltd., Mangr. J.B. Beale. Calcutta agents, Balmer, Lawrie and Co." Even in 1900 the garden is still called Bannockburn Tea Co. Ltd., and the only indications that the handover has taken place are the new manager Stanley D. Sinclair, Joachim Stölke's grandson, and the new Calcutta agents: Williamson, Magor & Co.

In 1901 at last the property becomes *"Bannockburn Tea Estate, Post Office Lebong ..... Proprtrs. F.J. & E.A. Wernicke; Mangr./Partner E.A. Wernicke"* — uncle and nephew in happy union!

From 1910 on, proprietors become "Mrs. E.A. Wernicke and others," though Ernest remains the manager.

The "*great amalgamation*" in 1919 included also Bannockburn, and just for this year it disappears from Thacker's list as an independent unit, and is found as part of the Lingia Tea Company Ltd. Strangely, however, it reappears as a seemingly independent estate as before, "*Proprs. Mrs. Wernicke and others; Mangr. E.A. Wernicke*" until Ernest's demise in May 1922. During the last year, Col. L. Hannagan was acting manager, then manager, and took over the final management whilst the heirs decided to dispose of the property. (His account of the Tea Industry in Darjeeling is reproduced in the appendix). The transfer must have taken place in 1923, as in the following year Bannockburn is no longer in the Directory.

And yet — it survived, for in a survey of 1981, the proprietors are Darjeeling Plantation Industries Ltd., with an acreage of 139.34 hectares (=56.39 acres) producing in 1979 a harvest of 79,722 kg. of leaves, and in 1980 an even better 80,090 kg. Only in shops specialising in "*Category 1*" quality teas is it possible to buy "Bannockburn!"

DEREK AND PANDAM

Fredrick (Fritz/Derrick) Page Wernicke — to give his full name ("Fritz" to his close relations) — was born at Darjeeling in 1877 and, like his brothers, educated at St. Paul's School. At the age of 17, in 1894, he was sent for further education to Cheltenham, together with his brother Frank, then aged 13, where he spent the next four years.

In 1898 Derrick, now 21, returned to Darjeeling and became an assistant at Lingia Tea Estate under the manager, Bruce Cowley, a cousin and son of Aunty Mary Cowley-Wernicke. The Cowley family had been "in tea" for a long time, and Uncle "Guss" and Cousin, Bruce, would have given Derrick four years of excellent training in the cultivation of the tea plant. In fact, the Cowleys lived at Marybong Tea Estate, right next door to Lingia.

The decisive year in Derrick's career was 1902, when he took over the management of Pandam Tea Estate from his elder brother, Ernest, who had been "superintending" the garden with the help of a manager (M.J. Flyter), and an assistant, (C.C. Marsden). The assistant stayed on for another year, no doubt to show Derrick "the ropes" of Pandam.

The "Pandam Tea Concern" had been acquired in 1888 (or 1889 — no records exist for this year) from its previous owners, the "Heirs of Munshee Mohamed Terequallah; manager Shamshere Ali". It appears in "Thackers Directory" for 1890 as "Pandam Tea Concern, acreage 200. Proprs. J.A. Warnicke and F.J. Warnicke. Manager R.K. Bose". By 1891, Thackers had discovered that the new owners were really Wernickes, and by 1892 the "Tea Concern" had become "Pandam Tea Estate".

The brothers, J.A. and F.J., however, were fully occupied with their other tea estates and, therefore, had to engage managers and assistants for Pandam. Fortunately, one family member or the other almost always seems to have been available to fill gaps, and brother-in-law "Gus" Cowley (father of Bruce) could look after Pandam. Things went well, and by 1895 the acreage had increased from 200 to 350 by adding Alubari North and Alubari South. The next three years saw two new managers, who temporarily prepared the way for Derrick's takeover in 1902.

A look at the Darjeeling map of 1933 reveals the favourable site of the Pandam Tea Gardens, whose tea bushes grew almost up to the Chowrasta, in easy reach of both the town centre for purchases and the railway station for despatch of the garden's product. Right opposite, and coming up the slope to the bazaar lies the Stölkes "Steinthal". It is not difficult to imagine the two families frequently meeting in town on shopping expeditions and, no doubt, paying a quick and loving visit to Grandmama (Sophie) Wernicke at Gloven.

Having worked for three years (1903-5) without an assistant, Derrick may have needed some help, and H.W. Onslow-Graham made his appearance for two years (1906-7), after which Derrick is left on his own, obviously running the estate smoothly and efficiently without the need of additional assistance, for the next 28 years (!) till 1936. It can only be hoped that he had an occasional holiday in all those years — but "Thackers Directory" would not know about that!

Two dates stand out in Derrick's professional progress: 1919 and 1925. 1919 was the year of the "great amalgamation" and restructuring of the Lingia Estate. Pandam ceased to be mentioned as an independent unit, and had become part of the newly-formed Lingia Tea Co. Ltd., and is, henceforth, quoted under this company. (See: Lingia Tea Estate). It was on this occasion that Derrick was given a seat on the board of directors. The second notable date was 1925, when he was elevated to "managing director", a position he held until his retirement in 1936. But the merger did not affect Derrick's appointment as manager of Pandam, where he stayed on to the end of his career.

It must have given Derrick great satisfaction and pleasure to welcome, during his last years as managing director, two of his nephews as assistants on the family tea gardens of Glenburn and Lingia: Cyril (Wrenick), son of brother Bernard (1931-37) and John (Warwick), son of brother Frank (1935-41). Both "boys" so much enjoyed their work that they stayed "in tea" for the rest of their lives.

It is interesting to note that although Derrick had changed his surname to Wren, as far as Thackers Directory was concerned he stayed with them to the end as he had started — F. Page Wernicke.

MARY

Mary Wernicke, sister of Andrew and Fred, helped extending "the Wernicke Empire" by marrying a Darjeeling tea planter, Patrick Augustus George Cowley, and thereby bringing in Marybong and Goomba tea estates as well as the Cowleys as partners in Lingia.

BRUCE COWLEY AND GLENBURN

Glenburn is supposed to have been bought at the same time as Bannockburn in 1895, but as in the case of the latter, the transfer of the property appears to have taken a long time, or Thackers were not well informed (which occasionally did happen). Whatever the circumstances, the Directory for 1897 supplied the following information: "Glenburn Tea Estate, Post Office Runjeet, Darjeeling; Gardens: Glenburn and Seembong (Kumbul). Acreage 350. Manager. James Macarthur; Assistant, Native. Calcutta agents, Williamson, Magor & Co." It was a peculiar custom of Thackers not to allow Indian assistants the dignity of a personal name; with a few exceptions they were just "natives."

During 1898 and 1899, C. H. Bald took over as manager, no doubt to the benifit of the estate, as he was an expert tea planter, who later wrote a standard work on the tea industry and every aspect of it.

In 1900 at last the family moves in, according to Thackers: "*Glenburn Tea Estate, Post Office Darjeeling … Proprs. J.W. Wernicke, F.J. Wernicke and M.M. Crawford (husband of Andrew's eldest daughter, Ethel). Mangr. F.A. Bruce Cowley (nephew, son of Andrew's sister, Mary).*"

Assistants changed rapidly over the next four years, and so did the *"logo"* of the garden after Andrew's death in 1904, the "W" losing its initials:

By 1905, the acreage of Glenburn and Suribong (=Seembong=Kumbul) has risen to 425, but the proprietors are now *"The Estate of the late J.A. Wernicke, F.J. Wernicke and M.M. Crawford"*; nephew Bruce Cowley continues as manager, in fact, he holds this position until 1917, and so Glenburn can be thought of as "his" tea garden.

In 1910 M.M. Crawford drops out as proprietor, but his place is taken by Dr. Jim (his brother) Crawford, and a new member of the Wernicke family is added: E.C. Onslow-Graham, son-in-law of Fred and husband of his daughter, Gertrude.

Nothing happens for the next few years until in 1918, the estate's acreage has risen to 575 (under the capable management of Bruce Cowley!) and a new manager, P.A. McNaught, who leads the estate into amalgamation with the Lingia Tea Co. Ltd. in 1919. Henceforth, Glenburn is no longer an independent unit but will be found under "Lingia" and the management of P.A. McNaught.

This is as good a place as any to tell the story of Malcolm M. Crawford, or Uncle Mac, as he was known to all the family, and most popular with all his nephews and nieces. How he came from Scotland to India is a tale of one shilling that turned into thousands! It runs like this: Young Malcolm was not keen on an academic career and so he was found a place in a bank. He was soon entrusted with looking after the cash till, and all went well until — one Saturday afternoon he wanted to see a football match, but discovered that he had left his purse at home and did not have the required shilling for the entrance fee. Unperturbed, he put his hand in his till and borrowed the shilling with the intention of putting it back first thing on Monday morning. Unfortunately, just that weekend a surprise check was made on his till, and it was found to be short of that one shilling. No explanations availed. Taking money without authorisation, however big or small a sum, was interpreted in those days as a plain and simple case of *"theft,"* and Malcolm was sacked that same Monday morning. He was thought of as having disgraced his family, and was regarded as the *"black sheep"* of the Crawfords. And they did what many families had done with their "black sheep" before, particularly in the 18th century; they packed him off to India.

What made Malcolm go to Darjeeling is not clear, but he did marry Ethel Wernicke, Andrew's eldest daughter, and became for some time, partner at Glenburn (succeeded by his brother Jim I.M.S. later on).

At around this time the Germans had invented aniline dyes, as a result of which the indigo industry in India collapsed, and one plantation after another had to close down and sell out. Land prices dropped to rock-bottom, and Malcolm bought up what he could. It is thought he turned to sugar and jute instead, and that is how one shilling turned into thousands at Shikarpur.

It seems that Uncle Mac had not really cared for tea anyhow, for one of his favourite pastimes was — pig-sticking, for which there was not much scope at Darjeeling. He founded the *"Shikarpur Hunt"* (blue coat with gilt buttons, with a boar's head embossed on them, and the letter S.H. This button was only given to a hunter after he had taken 20 "contested first spears"!). There were other serious rules, such as the prohibition to kill a sow or a boar under the length of 38 inches; offending "spears" were fined a dozen bottles of champagne after the hunt.

Malcolm kept an accurate record of who "stuck" what and when, and he came to the conclusion that "though there are varying degrees of excellence, these are all workmen. *"Not a man amongst them who cannot kill his boar fair and square single-handed, and this is as it should be"*.

The summary for five years (1904-1910) goes like this: 8 meetings, 21 days, average 12 *"spears"*. Average number of hogs killed per day 29, total 602; maximum number "struck" by one hunter 16, minimum 2. Malcolm usually got 7 and his total for these meetings comes to a moderate 32!

Malcolm was an extremely knowledgeable pig-sticker, and knew everything from the length and weight of the spear and the different shapes of spear-heads to the choice of hunting horse and the cunning and tricks of a boar, so much so that he was invited by Lieutenant-General Sir A.E. Wardrop to contribute a chapter of twenty pages on *"Pig-sticking in Bengal"* to a book on the subject of hog-hunting. Dear Uncle Mac!

Chapter 9

THE STÖLKES

The home of the Stölkes was in Germany, in the Brandenburg province, where they lived for generation after generation at Glöwen where they had a farm. There is still a road which passes the old Stölke farm, named after them - "Stölkenstrasse." The earliest Stölke that appears on the family tree is Menning [?] Stölke, 1696. The Stölke family were very closely associated with the Wernicke family at Klein Wulkow, about 30 km. distant, and there were three Stölke/Wernicke intermarriages - Joachim Stölke to Dorothea Sophia Wernicke in 1836, Johann Andreas Wernicke to Sophie Elizabeth Stölke in 1838 and Johann Christian Stölke, to Dorothea Wernicke some years after, as he was still in school when Sophie left for India. She briefly mentions him in her story "At Evening Time It Shall Be Light", when she says: "So with my younger brother Johannes, who was at school in Gnadau, I set off for Wulkow to say goodbye to Joachim." Of course we know that when she got there, she was offered a proposal of marriage by Joachim's friend, Andreas Wernicke so that she could also go out to India as a missionary. But years later, this younger brother Johannes, apparently also followed his sister's footsteps and joined up with the family in Darjeeling. What happened to him is a mystery. Did he take his wife to India? Did he stay in India? Did he return to Germany? Unfortunately, these will always remain unanswered questions. There are some references in Thackers for 1865 — 75 for a mysterious J. N. Stölke who was a Revenue Surveyor.

Joachim Stölke & Dorothea (nee Wernicke)

A few references are made with regard to Sophie's elder brother, Joachim, in her account "At Evening Time It Shall Be Light" — during their voyage, on their journey to Darjeeling and afterwards. Family links must have been very strong, indeed, because not only was Joachim her brother, but his wife was her husband's sister! But apart from these few references, not very much is known about Joachim and his family. The only reliable evidence are in letters he wrote back to his Mission in Germany.

Joachim and Dorothea had five children. The eldest was Maria, born about 1841, then came Mary Elizabeth, nicknamed "Bessie," on 2nd December 1842. After that two sons were born to them, John (about 1845) and William Joachim (about 1847), and finally, Dorothea Elizabeth (about 1850).

The family lived at "Steinthal" ("Stone Valley" in German), and the house is clearly marked on an old map of Darjeeling in 1862 as Mr. Stölke's. The house was located just below what is now the "*Lloyd Botanical Gardens,*" and was named "*Peace Valley.*" Another house, "*Rose Bank*" was later built, a little below and to one side of the first. The land he purchased was turned into a tea garden, "*Steinthal Tea Estate,*" and comprised only 45 acres. It may have been larger, originally, and there is some suggestion that part of the estate was taken over by the Government to build the Darjeeling Jail on the adjacent spur. Perhaps Joachim was paid something for this or given some land in exchange, for he then started another tea-garden, "*Risheehat*" of 160 acres below the Sukhiapokri Road that leads from Ghoom to the Singalila ridge, and onwards to Tonglu. Joachim was apparently the only one of the first generation of these German missionaries to start experimenting with tea-growing in the Darjeeling area, and "*Steinthal*" was probably one of the first of the tea-gardens started about 1850. Later generations of the Wernickes went "into tea" in quite a big way. Joachim died on the 10th June 1876 at age 67, and his wife died three years later.

Maria Stölke & Joseph Vaughn

The eldest of Joachim and Dorothea's daughters, Maria married a Joseph Vaughn in 1861, and they had one son (as far as records go) baptised "Joseph Charles Stölke-Vaughn" on 29th June 1862. This boy was later to marry his first cousin Dora (Daisy) Eleanor Sinclair in 1898, and it is strange how he and his wife laid claim to their uncles' John and William Stölke's estate (at least the money), while the brothers' sister, Dorothea was still alive, for in "The Probate of Administration" Rs. 1,13,037 was claimed by Joseph Charles Stölke-Vaughn, I.M.S. (India Medical Service) on William Stölke's estate, and Rs. 1,05,271 by his wife, Dora Eleanor Vaughn (née Stölke) on the estate of John.

Mary Elizabeth Stölke

The second of Joachim and Dorothea's daughters, she was betrothed to a William Sinclair but died at the age of 18, on 16th July 1861. There is a very poignant letter written by Andreas Wernicke to his sons in school in Calcutta on 10th July 1861, saying:

"Tell them [their cousins John and Willie who were also in school in Calcutta] that they shall look up to the Lord. It is His doing and we must submit, and that what he finds good for dear Mary shall also be good for us though we may not understand it at present but we shall in heaven praise Him for His works".

William married Mary's younger sister, who was only about 11 at the time of her sister's death, 4 years later.

John Stölke

Very, very little is known about John Stölke, Joachim and Dorothea's eldest son. Unfortunately, the Stölkes preserved little, if any, records of their life. Only the letters Joachim wrote back to his Mission still survive, and give a hint at the boy's character. He apparently wanted to study theology and become a missionary like his father, and seemed to be highly thought of by his headmaster. Alas, this wasn't to be, as far as we know, and he ended up too as a tea-planter, dying at Risheehat Tea Estate on 13th September 1911, aged about 66 years. He never married.

William Stölke

Baptised "Joachim William Stölke," he seemed to prefer to be called William, and was known as "Willie." Willie never "officially" married, but had a common-law Lepcha "wife" by whom he had several children — eleven of which are known, and two probable, as burial records show that two boys, Joachim and Richard Walter Stölke died aged 18 and 12 years as "students," so at least they were being educated. It is almost certain that they are Willie, and his Lepcha "wife" "Akhi's" children, as there were no other Stölke's about to generate any offspring, unless, as a "wide guess" they were the children of Sophie (and Joachim's) younger brother who "followed in her footsteps out to India".

The name of Willie's wife is shown as "Akhi" on one of their children's baptismal certificates and on another as "Lillian". This is not as strange as it seems, for many tea-planters who took local women or made them their wives gave them European names. However, it was not the "done thing" in India in those days, especially among the tea-planting community, and she could very well have been ostracised, though Willie himself could have been generally accepted. She was, after all, a simple native woman who to the end was loyal to her "husband". It is said that after Willie's death on the 17th of July 1911 (strangely only two months before his brother, John's death) she pined for him, and only lived for a few months afterwards, being cremated at Risheehat tea-estate. What happened to their many children afterwards is not clear. Whether they were allowed to continue to live on the property is not known. Most of them would have reached adulthood anyway, and some may have been in Calcutta. One was apparently working as a carriage inspector on the D. H. Railway.

The only "Stölkes" remaining in the Darjeeling District are a few of Willie's descendants. Father Benjamin Stölke was, perhaps, the last well-known member, living in Kalimpong where he was a Roman Catholic priest at St. Augustine's School till he died in the late 1960's. All the rest are scattered between the United Kingdom, Australia, and the United States.

Dorothea Stölke & William Sinclair

Dorothea was only about 11 years old when her elder sister, Mary (Bessie) died, while being betrothed to William Sinclair, and married William four years later when she was 15.

William Sinclair was the son of a John Sinclair who went out to India aged 17, as a soldier in the Horse Artillery in the days of the old East India Company, arriving there on 4th December 1820 on the *"George IV"* from Glasgow. During his career in the army, he rose to the rank of Sergeant at the time of his marriage to Mary Coyle, a widow, in 1832. He would have been 29 years of age by this time. On 1st December 1843 (at the age of 40) he was appointed Conductor with the Ordnance Commissariat Department of the Bengal Army, stationed at Cawnpore. The family comprised Mary and her two daughters by her previous marriage — and the other children by John, William and Janet. (There was an elder boy, also called John, but he died aged 15 and is buried beside his father in the Kacheri Cemetery, Cawnpore). John Sinclair died in 1848 aged 45, and the family continued to live in Cawnpore thereafter, until the terrible events of 1857 — The Indian Mutiny.

William must have been about 19 yrs. at that time and his sister, 17. It is not known whether their mother, Mary, had remarried or not, or whether, she had, indeed, died by then. In any case, all their fates were overtaken by events, for in the first week of June, General Wheeler's entrenchment, where about 1,500 Europeans and Eurasian residents of Cawnpore took refuge, came under siege by the rebels. What followed were days and days of constant bombardment, intolerable heat, and death, till on June 27th on the promise of safe conduct to Calcutta via the Ganges river, these poor unfortunates were massacred at Sati Chowra Ghat as they were beginning to board the boats which were to take them to safety. The surviving women and children, about 200 in all, were held in the Bibi Ghur — the former residence of a British "nabob" for his native women. Here William's sister was to perish in the bloodbath that followed on the 15th of July, when all the women and children were butchered. Her name is listed among the dead as "Miss Sinclair."

Amazingly William survived! How, we do not know, except that according to "family legend" he disguised himself as a native and escaped Cawnpore. This was almost miraculous, because he was "presumed dead," and an entry for a "Mr. Sinclair of E.I. Railways," appears on Jonah Shepherd's list of those who died at Sati Chowra Ghat on 27th June. It is all the more strange, because William's brother-in-law, Matthew Ogle (married to his half-sister — Mary's daughter by her first husband) may have been similarly disguised, when he was caught and killed, as historian Andrew Ward writes in his book on the Cawnpore Massacres, "*Our Bones Are Scattered*": "Other fugitives were not so lucky. Sergeant Matthew Ogle of the Canal Department was captured and killed after trying to escape into the countryside."

It is not known when William made his bid for freedom. He was most likely working with the East Indian Railways, possibly as a junior surveyor, and the surveyors were a great help in defending Wheeler's entrenchment, as also noted by Andrew Ward in his book. It is possible that he escaped Cawnpore before events took a really nasty turn, but even so, to escape through a hostile countryside was not without its risks. But why William never wrote an account of his experiences is a mystery till this day. To survive Cawnpore was very rare indeed, as only about a dozen or so known Europeans and Eurasians "lived to tell the tale" out of the 1,500 original residents, including poor Matthew Ogle's wife and "large family." What is so poignant was that their last baby boy, Arthur Sinclair Ogle, was only born to them on the 22nd January of that fateful year. Perhaps William felt terrible guilt that all of his kith and kin had perished, and that he had escaped Cawnpore in a not very chivalrous way.

Whatever, William seemed determined to marry into the Stölke family! He was patient enough to wait 4 years since the death of "his beloved" Bessie in order that Dorothea reach "marriageable age" (15 at that time), and must have kept close links with the Darjeeling family. He married Dorothea on 31st August 1865 at Darjeeling (where else?) and is described as "A Surveyor" on the marriage certificate. They had 8 children — Eleanor (1866) of whom not much is known, Mabel (1868 — she committed suicide at Risheehat in 1899 by taking an overdose of laudanum), William Duncan (1870 — he died as an infant aged 6 months), Norman William Patterson (1871 — he married a Julia Fink and had three daughters by her), Stanley Donald Stölke Sinclair (1872 — he married a German lady, Eleanor Haegert and had a son Tracy George and a daughter Cicely by her), Dudley Edward Patterson (1874 — he died aged 5 by falling from a tree), Dora (Daisy) Eleanor (1878 — she married her first cousin, her Aunt Maria Stölke's son,

Joseph Charles Stölke Vaughn) and finally Violet Mildred (1888 — she married a Thomas Mackenzie). It is interesting to note how "Stölke" is preserved in both Stanley Sinclair and his cousin Joseph Vaughn's names, probably in honour of Joachim Stölke, as the name was about to die out, seeing that neither of his sons had married (or at least "properly" married!).

William is shown in various entries in Thackers, sometimes being referred to as proprietor of Risheehat (1881) and Steinthal (1891) so he probably owned shares in the gardens. However, the two families — the Stölkes and Wernickes seemed to drift apart with the coming of the "new generation". How often the families saw each other is not well known. Whether this "drifting apart" took place earlier, after Joachim and Sophie's children had grown up is quite likely. Certainly, there is mention of the "close links" at the time of Mary Stölke's death in 1861, when the 2nd generation were growing to adulthood. Perhaps it may have been Willie's liaison with a local girl that caused the rift. We do not know. But there was a great lack of contact between the two families in the 3rd generation. There may have been other reasons though; the Darjeeling District was quite widespread, and the tea-gardens often lay at great distances from each other. Transport was always a problem — pony traps and the likes were unsuitable for the terrain, so horse-riding and "shank's pony" were the only means of getting around. It is likely that the families met at important events, such as christening's, weddings and funerals. In regard to Christenings, there is a poignant document (Baptismal Certificate) where Joachim Stölke is called to baptise Andrea's and Sophie's little baby who was not expected to survive the day. The entry says: "Baptised by Mr. Stölke privately. Child being in danger and Chaplain unwell". The child, Auguste Wernicke, was born on 15th September 1854 and died the same day.

The Third Generation

After the death of Dorothea Sinclair (Stölke) on 4th August 1914, (her husband William Sinclair had died in 1907) the two Stölke tea-gardens were divided up amongst the surviving family. It seemed that Norman, Stanley and Dora (Daisy) were the more active shareholders in the gardens. Norman looked after Risheehat and Stanley looked after Steinthal. But it was decided, on Dorothea's death, that Steinthal be sold. Stanley's sister, Dora, was "after buying it", but Stanley put his bid in first, so a great rift took place within the Sinclair family and Dora (Daisy) had no further contact with her brother and his family, although in later years, Stanley's children, Tracy George and Cicely became in contact with Dora's family (Geoffrey, Theo and Gwynedd) once again. Norman's children were, however, much closer to Stanley's, and they often used to spend their Christmases at Risheehot. But Norman gave up management of Risheehat, and it was sold off in the 1930's, when he and his family left for England, followed by his sister Dora (Daisy) and her family.

Fortunes for the Sinclair's began to change at around about that time too. Stanley's wife, Eleanor Haegert had died in 1918. Unable to look after his two children, Tracy George and Cicely, he employed a governess, a Miss Wilks, to look after them, and ended up marrying her. He had several children by this second marriage, but, like the mists that rise up suddenly from the valleys of Darjeeling, the "weather" began to take a nasty turn. Stanley had to take out a large loan from a local Indian businessman to modernise the factory machinery. There was heavy interest to be paid on this loan, and the tea-garden was not large enough to give Stanley the required turnover to make a profit and pay off the loan at the same time. Eventually, the money-lender foreclosed, and the family were forced to leave the property and live in Sonada and Tung. By this time, his eldest son, Tracy George had married, as had his daughter Cicely. But there was still the rest of the family to provide for, so their circumstances were impoverished, indeed. Eventually, Stanley died from heart failure on the 16th February 1938 and was buried in the Singtom Cemetery. All his children from both marriages left India by 1949.

Finis

A BRIEF BIBLIOGRAPHY OF SOME RELEVANT BOOKS ON DARJEELING

GERHARD, PAUL. UM DEN ABEND WIRD ES LICHT SEIN! Die Lebensgeschichte einer 85 jährigen Missionärswitwe. *pub. Evangelische Buchhandlung, Breslau 1904. Translated by Timothy Davies & privately published as "At Evening Time it Shall be Light", in 1996*

THE DORJEELING GUIDE. PUB. SMITH, CALCUTTA 1845.

BHANJA, DR. K.C. DARJEELING AT A GLANCE. *pub Darjeeling 1941*

BHANJA, DR. K.C. WONDERS OF DARJEELING AND THE SIKKIM HIMALAYA. *pub. Gilbert, Darjeeling 1943.*

BUCHANAN, W.J. NOTES ON OLD DARJEELING, *Bengal Past & Present, vol 2 1908.*

BROWN, PERCY. TOURS IN SIKKIM AND THE DARJEELING DISTRICT. *pub. Newman, Calcutta 1917.*

CAMPBELL, A. NOTES ON THE LEPCHAS OF SIKKIM *with a vocabulary of their Language. Journal of the Asiatic Society of Bengal, 9 (1940), 379-93.*

CAMPBELL FORRESTER, J. THE SANCTUARY OF THE HIMALAYAS. *pub. Calcutta 1920. Darjeeling, Calcutta Review, 28. (1857)*

DARJEELING IN 1841, BY J.D. *Bengal Past & Present, vol.44 (1932)*

DASH, A.J. ED. BENGAL DISTRICT GAZETTEERS: DARJEELING. *pub. Alipore 1947*

DOZEY, E.C. A CONCISE HISTORY OF DARJEELING DISTRICT. *pub. Mukherjee, Calcutta 1922.*

EDGAR, J.W. REPORT ON A VISIT TO SIKHIM AND THE THIBETAN FRONTIER IN OCTOBER, NOVEMBER & DECEMBER 1873. *pub Calcutta 1873.*

HOOKER, J.D. HIMALAYAN JOURNALS. *pub. J. Murray 1854.*

MUKHERJEE, B. & MERCER, A. A SHORT HISTORY OF DARJEELING DISTRICT. *pub. Kurseong 1962*

NEWMAN'S GUIDE TO DARJEELING & NEIGHBOURHOOD. *pub. Calcutta 1919*

O'MALLEY DISTRICT GAZETTEER DARJEELING, pub.Darjeeling. 1907. *rpt. New Delhi: Logos Press.*

RISLEY, H.H. (ED.) THE GAZETTEER OF SIKHIM. *Calcutta. 1894.*

OTHER BOOKS BY FRED PINN

SEASHELLS OF EAST AFRICA. *pub. Rex Collings, London 1977.*

A FIRST GUIDE TO THE INDIAN OCEAN SEASHORE. *pub. OUP, Nairobi 1973.*

THE ROAD OF DESTINY. DARJEELING LETTERS 1839. *pub. OUP Calcutta 1986.*

LOUIS MANDELLI Darjeeling Tea Planter & Ornithologist. *priv.pub 1985.*

SEA SNAILS OF PONDICHERRY. *pub. Nehru Science Centre Pondicherry 1990.*

TRAVELLING TO DARJEELING IN 1861. *ed by Fred Pinn, priv. pub. Darjeeling*

TRAVELLING TO DARJEELING IN 1830 *BY CAPT. J. HERBERT, ed. by Fred Pinn.(reprint of the 1831 articles in the Journal of the Asiatic Society).Pub. Pagoda Tree Press, Bath. 1999.*

Appendix. 1.

<u>Darjeeling Planting -Then and Now.</u>

by
Lt. Col. L Hannagan, E.D., F.R.H.S.

_____

<u>Mr. James Andrew Wernicke</u>

When James Andrew Wernicke arrived in Darjeeling with the band of German Missionaries who joined Mr. Stark at the Tukvar Mission in 1841, he was only a few months old, and thus we can rightly describe him as having grown up with the Town and District of Darjeeling. We have already recounted how the Tukvar Mission failed, and how the missionaries moved to the town of Darjeeling and were compelled by the gradual suspension of their funds to seek various means of earning an honest livelihood whilst continuing their mission work.

The dire struggle for existence which these families endured can be imagined if we remember that they were foreigners in a strange land, remote from civilization, isolated and cut off from the world, as it was then, by forests and large rivers, with communications, roads, and travel facilities that were, indeed, hazardous and primitive. They lived like Spartans strong in their faith in God and themselves and whilst they eked out a precarious existence by petty trading, teaching and tilling the soil, they made a thorough study of the customs and languages of the hill peoples.

What was it that kept these families in Darjeeling? Perhaps, after their experiences in war-torn Europe, they found it a haven of peace from the turbulence and distress of the civilized world - a Garden of Eden! Perhaps, to them, Darjeeling, in the words of John Milton, "It was a place chosen by the sovran Planter, when he framed all things to Man's delightful use".

It was in these surroundings and under these conditions that J.A. Wernicke grew up. He was commonly known as Andrew Wernicke, and his eldest son, Ernest Andrew Wernicke, who, for many years was managing proprietor of the Bannockburn Tea Estate until his death in 1922, was commonly called Ernest Wernicke. But to the hill people they were always affectionately known as "Jetta Sahib".

Through his nationality and upbringing, Andrew Wernicke possessed the gift of languages. Besides German and English, he was a scholar of Latin and Greek, and he spoke ou understood most of the hill languages and dialects. He became so proficient in the latter, that later in his life, when an Honorary Magistrate, it was said that he seldom required an interpreter in Court.

At an early age, Andrew Wernicke displayed an interest in the church, and destined to take holy orders, and he was actually working for the B.A. degree at Bishop's College, Calcutta, when towards the end of 1863 he was informed of the sudden death of his father, and was compelled to break off his studies and return to Darjeeling.

He was now faced with the problem of earning his own living in order to support his widowed mother and her family, who were financially very badly off. His younger brother, Fred Wernicke, was already an assistant at Soom Tea Estate, which at that time belonged to a Captain Jerdon; but salaries were then very small, and it was obvious that Andrew Wernicke should add his quota to the family exchequer.

He immediately applied for and was given the job of an assistant on Captain Masson's estates at Tukvar (Tukvar Tea Co.) but for some appreciable time after, he still hankered after the church, though in due course the pressure of family circumstances and a growing love of tea planting, forced him to relinquish this ambition. Nevertheless, he continued his studies for the priesthood for many months after entering Tea, and copies of two letters, which follow, are quoted in support of this statement.

The first is dated Bishop's College, 29th January, 1864 and is addressed to Andrew Wernicke by the Principal, a Dr. Kay. It goes: "Next month (23rd Feb.) I am to leave, D.V. for England. Before leaving, let me send a line to say I should like to know how you have been getting on since you left. I hope you have not wholly given up the prospect of being some time a minister of the Gospel". And the second letter from the Rev. W. G. Cowie, Bishop's Chaplain, Bishop's Palace, Calcutta, and dated 15th April 1864, reads: "... the Bishop desires me to send you a copy of his Lordship's 'Suggestions' to the Clergy, in which you will find, at pp. 33,34 a list of the subjects of examination for Deacon's Orders. If you have more than sufficient time for preparing the special subjects, you should go on reading as much of the Greek Testament as you can".

Throughout his life, Andrew Wernicke maintained an unsectarian enthusiasm for church and chapel, and a keen interest and a warm enthusiasm for education. During his life, he was a handsome donor to St. Paul's School, Darjeeling. He was a man of clear perception and great determination, and did not spare himself in his work. Tea planting in those days was a particularly arduous job, entailing long hours in the field beginning at dawn and ending with dusk, and during the hours of working all meals, whether in rainy or in fine weather, were taken on the job. In those early days of Darjeeling Planting, it was men like Andrew and Fred Wernicke and George Watt Christison, who learnt the hard way, and later set the standard and the duties of future generations of Darjeeling Planters.

Andrew Wernicke was 23 years of age when he entered Tea, and during the two years he was at Tukvar, he planted out the "fourth division", which at the time of his death over forty years later, remained the finest piece of tea planting in that Company.

These early planters had to be "Jacks of all Trades", as they were on the outskirts of civilization, and had to manage all their problems themselves and without the help o technical experts and scientific officers. They literally managed on "the smell of an oil-rag", and this taught them to eschew blue prints and high sounding theories and stick to hard practice and proved observation. They had to aquire, if they did not already possess it, a rough elementary knowledge of machinery and building, the making of tools and equipment, how to repair any breakages, how to improvise with the materials at hand in an emergency, for the coolie was primitively rustic and had only been taught to watch a wheel go round, and stop it at regular intervals. The planter would have to do his own plumbing and sanitation, his own engineering and construct his own buildings. He had to be a bit of a surveyor, as most roads were inclined to follow goat tracks and woodcutters paths, and hillsides were steep and cut up by marshes and deep ravines, large boulders and precipices. He had to study the transport of his crop, and be an accountant to keep his own books, a little bit of a lawyer, and even a judge to settle the disputes that would arise.

In those early days of Darjeeling Planting, racial hatreds and national bigotry were non-existent, and the simple hill-people were quick to realise and appreciate the organising ability, the integrity and justice of the white man. Moreover, it was an important feature of British policy., that the planter had to keep up the white man's reputation for justice and fair dealings, which would require hours of patient hearing of a dispute, and then a just and equitable settlement. More often than not, such disputes if complicated, were settled by panchayet, with the planter acting as a neutral chairman.

Perhaps one of the best examples of the good fellowship which existed then between the planters and the hill-people is the following story which the author was told by the late Ernest Wernicke. When Lingia first came into being as a tea garden, his uncle, Fred Wernicke, would often on a warm summer's evening after a long and tiring day in the field and factory, sit on his factory steps and enjoy the last of the sunshine while he pondered on his problems and work. He was a young man then and a bachelor. On many an occasion, he would be joined by one of his teamakers who was having a few minutes rest form his work, and they would sit side by side discussing the work or village problems. On one occasion, a friend who suffered from an over-rated sense of his own importance, and never permitted such 'liberties', was horrified when a teamaker came out, sat down by Fred Wernicke, put his arm round his shoulder and gave him an affectionate hug, and addressed him as 'Daduu' or brother.

The courage and endurance of the early pioneers is well illustrated in the following description of an accident Andrew Wernicke suffered during his employment at Tukvar, and which is quoted from the notes of his son, Colonel Frank Warnick, late Indian Medical Service:

"While father was at Tukvar, he had the great misfortune to meet with a gun accident. Using an old-fashioned muzzle-loader gun, he returned to his bungalow from green-pigeon shooting. The gun had been wetted by rain. Resting the gun on the edge of the bed, he was wiping it down when it slipped to the floor and, exploding with the concussion, discharged the shot, which shattered the left hand and wrist. He must have suffered great pain, for I believe that it was not till the following day that arrangements could be made to carry him in a dandy to Darjeeling, where the arm was amputated below the elbow. In spite of this handicap, father used to ride everywhere up and down the hills on his ponies, and he also enjoyed an occasional shot with his old gun, and many a game of billiards, resting the cue at the elbow joint or using a billiards rest."

On leaving Tukvar at the end of 1865, Andrew Wernicke was given the management of Makaibaree Tea Estate (Kurseong &Darjeeling Tea Col., which comprised Makaibaree, Kelabaree-the beginning of the present Long View, and Aloobaree - the present Pandam), which with the other Tukvar (now of the Lebong Co. and five years the younger of the two) and managed by G.W. Christison, were the first Darjeeling gardens worked to a profit. Thus, in 1867, Andrew Wernicke and G.W. Christison were the first to demonstrate that tea gardens on the hills would be remunerative if worked with the most careful economy and industry, thereby leading the forlorn hope of tea, as it were, when such older tea pioneers as Hallifax and Harrold had actually withdrawn for a time, apparently despairing of its success in the hills.

Two years later, on the 6th December, 1867, Andrew Wernicke married Miss Niebel at the Baptist Chapel, Monghyr, in the plains, where the family had moved from Darjeeling after the death of Carl Gotleb Niebel, a member of the German missionary band at Tukvar.

It was between the years 1865 and 1867 that the two brothers, Andrew and Fred Wernicke, began to realise that any improvement in their financial status could only be brought about by launching out on their own as independent owners of tea gardens, and in reaching this decision they were undoubtedly encouraged by the anxiety of the Government to develop the tea industry in the hills, and was offering land at quite nominal freehold prices to anyone with experience of tea planting and manufacture. In due course, they acquired the land at Lingia, comprising some 550 acres for the price of Rs. 600/- (£40/-).

At that time, the land was probably under native cultivation (chiefly maize and kodo) and partly jungle, and work had to begin from scratch. The first tea was put out by an ex-sergeant round where the manager's house now stands, Fred Wernicke coming over from Soom to supervise the work. The two brothers worked in a close partnership, supervising the terracing of the hillsides to prevent rain-erosion, and planting of the new tea from established nurseries or seed at stake.

Shortly after work on Lingia was satisfactorily taking shape, the neighbouring spur of Tumsong was acquired as a free gift from the Government, and was laid out on similar lines as a tea garden - Tumsong covered some 440 acres. Both gardens were some 12 to 15 miles from Darjeeling, the elevation varying from the top to the bottom of the gardens by some 2000 to 3000 feet. The temperatures at the foot of the gardens made it possible to establish small fruit-orchards containing bananas, guavas, oranges and pineapples. Most of the early gardens of Darjeeling have similar orchards at their lowest elevations.

At the same time, a system of roads and bridle-paths was planned and built to enable labour to get readily about the estate and to facilitate the removal of leaf to the factory-site. This road building by tea garden owners had also to include the opening of communications between the gardens and the outside world for many miles. Many of these roads outside the gardens were later taken over by the P.W.D., and District Board, and were so carefully surveyed and laid out by the original pioneers that today few alterations have been necessary to convert them inot motorable roads.

A curious feature of the District Board Roads which run through or outside the tea gardens of the District of Darjeeling is that they are still maintained by Honorary Contractors appointed by the Board, and in the majority of cases the Honorary Contractors were and still are planters, for although Indian representation on this Board is in the main Indian (Bengali, Marwari, and Hill People) they still trust the planter and appreciate his integrity and skill in maintaining the roads in the best possible condition with the very limited funds available. And, although the cost of living in the District has risen very many times in the past fifty years, the funds allocated by the Board to its roads remain unaltered, save in respect of motorable roads where special allowances are made according to their importance or usefulness.

It soon became evident to the brothers Wernicke that remote control of their properties was unsatisfactory, as, above all, it was impossible to keep an accurate check on expenditure, and so in 1866 or 1867, Mr. Fred Wernicke left Soom to personally control the work at Lingia. At first he lived in a small roughly-built bungalow, in reality a 'glorified' coolie hut with a thatched roof, watching over the building of the factory and work on the garden.

It must be remembered that the opening of Lingia and Tumsong was a bold and hazardous venture, and it was only by exercising the most rigid economies and sacrificing even the simplest luxuries, which today might be considered to be necessaries, that the two brothers were able to achieve their objective. For instance, when first building the factory, cement, corrugated iron and steel girders and beams were quite beyond their means, so the walls were made of sun-dried bricks, the foundations of stone and mud, the floors of soorki, a composition of quicklime and sand, and the roof elements and windows were of wood, all prepared from materials on the garden. The roof itself was thatched.

As Colonel Warwick puts it: "These must have been lean years indeed, waiting for the first returns from the sale of their teas. Their labour and the self-denial of those early years was amply rewarded later with success such as they could never have dreamed of, so that these sons of poor stranded German missionaries were able to send their own children to England and have them educated at well-known public schools, and enable them to enjoy so many things which their fathers and mothers had never known or thought possible in these days of their early struggles".

In 1873, Andrew Wernicke left Makaibaree, and with his wife and two young children, Ethel and Ernest (later managing proprietor of Bannockburn and Tumsong) joined Fred Wernicke at Lingia. Fred Wernicke was still a bachelor, but even so, his bungalow was too cramped for the others, who accommodated themselves for the first winter in the factory itself, occupying the long upstairs withering loft, which ran the length of the factory, and was divided by "light partitions into bedrooms and a bathroom, and meals were taken in one of the downstairs rooms of the factory. All water had to be carried by hand from a nearby stream (which was the beginning of the use of a bhisti or paniwallah), and lamps and candles provided light at night."

That winter was a very busy one for the brothers, for in addition to pushing on with the building of the manager's house, which was designed to accommodate both families, considerable thought and care had to be exercised in preparing the Lingia tea for the new season's cropping and manufacture, as Lingia now constituted the keystone of their future prosperity, and at the same time plans were prepared for a factory and bungalow or house at Tumsong, and the planting of tea on that property was speeded up.

By the spring of 1874, the new house at Lingia was completed, and they all moved across to occupy it. Fred Wernicke had married a Miss Hannah Lindeman, neice to the Rev. Niebel, in the previous year, and it was now possible for him to bring his bride to live at Lingia. Unfortunately, their first-born a boy born in November, 1878, only survived a few weeks, and his death was a great grief to both parents. Their remaining two children, Winifred and Gertrude were born in 1879 and 1881.

By 1876, Lingia and Tumsong had reached a stage in their development when it became obvious to the brothers that, working them conjointly from Lingia, which in the beginning had been found so economical and convenient, especially in regard to supervision, was now proving expensive and cumbersome, and that the sooner the gardens were made entirely separate properties, the better.

The Wernicke economy, both in regard to their private living, and in matters of business such as in the maintenance of house property and the working and expenditure of their tea gardens, was, and probably still is based on the maxim that one must always "cut one's coat according to one's cloth". At that time, in the 1870's mechanical inventions and ingenuity for interlocking large tea areas did not exist, and the small self-contained tea garden of 300 to 400 acres if tea land seemed the best commercial proposition. Even in the present highly advanced mechanical age, it is doubtful or problematic whether owing to the perishable quality of tea leaf, tea factories, however well equipped, can cope satisfactorily with the leaf of over 600 acres of tea land. There are, of course, exceptions where ideal conditions of growth, topography, climate, situation, etc., facilitate the maintenance of one central factory for an even larger area of tea land, but practice and, perhaps nature also may support our question, for if the average acreage of all tea gardens in North-East India was calculated, it would be found to be very near 600 acres.

In 1876, the Wernickes had already discovered that Darjeeling teas possessed something which was very rare in the world of their time, and is by no means common today, and this is the intrinsic flavour of teas grown at high altitudes and in particular aspects. They were also beginning to find out for themselves how elusive flavour in tea can be, and how easily it is lost by damage to leaf in transport over long distances and in stuffy baskets. Moreover, their experience at Soom, Tukvar, Makaibaree, Lingia and Tumsong had given them a certain understanding of the division between the accepted physical characteristics or standard of quality and the lesser known ethereal characteristics or attributes of flavour. They were aware of differences in flavour between individual gardens and districts or sub-districts. They were already beginning to recognize the differing flavours by such terms as 'lemon', 'strawberry', 'muscatel', etc., and they knew that a blend of two distinctive flavours produced an unrecognizable and not very desirable bastard.

At that time, pack pony transport and wire leaf shoots had not been thought of, and the pluckers had to carry their leaf to the factory in their own leaf baskets. The tea sections of Lingia were all within easy walking distances from the factory, but those at Tumsong were much further away, and the pluckers had often an hour's walk across to Lingia factory at the end of a long and tiring day's plucking. Naturally, the sections of Tumsong farthest from the Lingia factory and at the lowest and warmest altitudes were the first to mature, and so most of the leaf from this garden arrived in a semi-withered, and some in a semi-fermented condition. Besides, the pluckers of the Tumsong leaf were never pleased to see the Lingia pluckers walking home a comfortable half-hour or more before them.

When the factory at Lingia was planned some estimate of the crop it would have to deal with had been estimated, but such calculations were pure guesswork, as nobody yet knew the full bearing capacity of tea at high altitudes. It was becoming increasingly evident in 1876 that the Lingia factory could hardly cope with its own crop, and as increasing quantities of leaf began pouring in daily from Tumsong, the need for an extension to the factory, or a separate factory at Tumsong, became urgent.

The question of the division of labour between the gardens was also becoming increasingly important. At that time, some labour was resident on both gardens, more at Lingia than at Tumsong, but still a good deal of labour had to be employed from the bustees and khas mahals outside the properties. Labour was switched from one garden to the other according to immediate requirements. Labour employed on field works received contract rates and naturally preferred work which entailed minimum effort for the rates paid. The casual or outside labourers were very independent, and if they did not like a particular job they simply did not turn up for it. For instance, a piece of easy sickling or a good leaf flush offering extra overtime was a far more attractive proposition than a long day thullying (weeding), or tipping young tea. The young tea had to be tipped or thullied, and the mature flush had to plucked, so often the two jobs were combined, a condition of work on an easier or more paying job being first, some time in doing the more difficult or less lucrative job. Thus there was quite a lot of overlapping of work between the gardens which it was difficult to assess and separate out.

The late Ernest Wernicke, eldest son of Andrew Wernicke, who remembered many of the incidents of those early times, used to recount how a batch of sicklers from the khas mahal some four or five miles away, would arrive at a section by 7 a.m., each sickle his allotted third of an acre of tea land, and be wending their way home again by 10 a.m. One of those young sicklers became his paniwallah, then his cook, first at Tumsong, later at Bannockburn, and when Ernest Wernicke died in 1922, old Kancha Rai was not only cook, but the most important Coolie Sirdar and Contractor on the estate as well as "Jetta Sahib's" guide and counsellor in labour matters, and he also had a quiet and effective way of dealing with young Assistants who might be too impetuous or headstrong in their behaviour towards the labour.

There can be no doubt that the division of Lingia and Tumsong received very careful consideration before it was carried out, as these were indeed anxious years for the brothers and their families. Money was extremely tight, and one can imagine how they scraped and saved to carry on, pooling their meagre resources, denying all luxuries or wasteful fancies, plotting and planning ahead, ever cautious or over-optimism, and only spending when and where results seemed reasonably certain.

Their first venture into the realms of tea proprietorship had been born from the dire necessity of securing the life line of survival; their second venture into the Caesarian operation which brought Lingia and Tumsong into existence as separate self-contained tea properties was even more daring, but now they had a measure of past achievement and success to back them, and a clearer perception of the difficulties to be overcome.

And so Tumsong came to have its own factory, its own labour force, both resident and outside the garden, and its own separate existence as a tea property. By 1877, the factory and godowns had been built and were in operation, and by the end of the winter of 1878/79 the manager's bungalow was ready for occupation, and Andrew Wernicke and his family moved over to it from Lingia.

During the time he had been sharing the Lingia bungalow, three more children, Bernard, Henry and Derick (F. Page Wernicke who later managed Pandam, and was a Director of the Lingia Tea Company till his retirement just before World War II). In 1881 and 1893, two more sons, Frank and Wilfred were added to the family.

Years of privation combined with long hours of toil in all weathers now began to affect his health, and in 1881, Andrew Wernicke was obliged through ill-health to relinquish the management of Tumsong for a year or two and retire to Darjeeling. As soon as he was better, however, he returned to Tumsong, but this proved too much for him, and about 1884 he gave up active tea planting for good, and the whole family finally took up residence at "Willow Dale", old Grandfather Wernicke's house. Fred Wernicke, however, continued to live and work at Lingia for some years after Andrew's retirement, but eventually, crippled with rheumatism and arthritis, he retired himself about ten years later.

For Andrew Wernicke retirement from active tea garden management was only a step to even greater activities on a wider scale, for he had now to think of his children's education. By 1885, Darjeeling had become a popular hill resort for visitors and tourists thanks to the Darjeeling Himalayan Railway, and Europeans working in Calcutta and in the plains of Bengal, Bihar and Assam, also rich Indians and Maharajahs had begun sending their wives and children to it during the hot months of the Indian Summer. House property boomed, and Andrew Wernicke was not slow in taking advantage of this new means of increasing his income. "Holmdene" and "Midwood" were built, the former as a more commodious residence for the family. In 1892, the family took up residence at "Holmdene", and "Midwood" and "Willowdale" were leased out to suitable tenants. Later other houses were added, and in 1895 the two brothers acquired Glenburn and Bannockburn Tea Estates, and a year or two later, Pandam Tea Estate. These properties were purchased by means of borrowing, such was their credit with local banks and their faith in the future of Darjeeling tea. Nevertheless, the repayment of these loans was a cause of much anxiety and sacrifice for many years afterwards.

Colonel F. Warwick describes the taking over of Pandam in these words: "On our arrival at the factory, father was asked by some of the old factory hands to give them a sign by which they might recognise his authority of ownership of the new garden. This father did by breaking a branch from a tree, and thus proved that he was master and could do as he liked to his own property, and this simple procedure was enough to satisfy them".

The local government officials were quick to appreciate Andrew Wernicke's calm, judicial mind and public spirit by making him an Honorary Magistrate, a position he held for nearly thirty-five years, much of the time with first-class powers, and at one time he was the sole Honorary Magistrate and Municipal authority at Kurseong, besides being a Municipal Commissioner of Darjeeling Town.

His interest in the communications of the District also received recognition, and for many years, and until his death in 1904, he was Vice-Chairman of the District Road Cess Committee. In fact he was responsible for the original survey and alignment of many of the existing District Board Roads, and there is alive today a very ancient Cooly Sirdar of Margaret's Hope Tea Estate, who could remember seeing Andrew Wernicke, or "Jetta Sahib" as he called him, patiently supervising the alignment and construction of a District Board Road in the Kurseong Sub-Division. These public services were voluntary and unpaid.

There is no doubt that, through his free Public Service, he sought to make some return to the district and the people in gratitude for the opportunities they had allowed him to make good in his own private affairs. Unostentatious and retiring by nature, he avoided the limelight and on the rare occasions when he was asked to speak in public, was readier to acclaim the efforts of others than speak of his own achievements, and today the only reminder of him is a scruffy path linking the Auckland Road with the old Tonga Road and called Wernicke Road. Yet he once generously offered Rs.50,000 to the Darjeeling Municipality on condition that the grand central location should be secured as a public park for the town, and had this offer been accepted and backed, the present minature park below St. Andrew's Church would have extended from Government House to the Chowrasts, and given Darjeeling a coronet more worthy of the Queen of Hill Stations than the present ugly conglomeration of roof tops.

His love for trees made Andrew Wernicke a lifelong enemy of deforestation, and on his own properites, and those later managed by his sons, Ernest and Derick, the forest lands were amongst the best in the district. Their policy was "live and let live" and the extraction of forest produce was always on a selective basis. They were always drumming it into their Assistants and Staffs that one should copy Nature in dealing with Nature and that one could destroy in a few minutes what it took Nature ten, fifteen or twenty years to grow. The gaping scars and wastes of scrub land which now disfigure the mountain sides of Darjeeling are ample vindication of the soundness of forest treatment by men such as the Wernickes, G.W. Christison, and J.G.D. Cruickshank, and bear silent though tortured witness to the folly of clear felling which so many planters have thoughtlessly followed through the years.

Andrew Wernicke also worked hard to check the abuses of native cultivation on his properites, and he encouraged his workers to maintain the terraces and drains in their khetland in good order, and to strengthen them with fodder and fruit trees.

At his death in 1904 he had the joy of knowing that all his "ships" had come safely home, and his public obituary described him as "a prudent counsellor, always conciliatory, he was possessed of many qualities the district can ill spare".

Early Manufacture

By the time the Lingia factory was built, about 1870, tea manufacture had advanced from the primitive methods of repeated pannings, rollings, sun-dryings, and firings to a more standardised system of withering, rolling, fermenting and firing, but machinery as employed today, or even as employed in the 1890's, was unheard of , and, anyway, even in Assam it was purely experimental in efforts to simplify the rolling and drying processes. In fact, even until 1880, all teas in Darjeeling were handmade.

A number of people had written about Chinese tea manufacture, but, perhaps with the exception of Robert Fortune, they had not actually witnessed the process, and their accounts were entirely based on hearsay. There was the Dutchman, Jacobson, who wrote about it in 1843, and Samuel Ball, who described the preparation of tea in 1848 from notes he had made at Canton twenty years earlier, and Robert Fortune's account came out in 1852. From all these accounts it was clear that there was no fixe standard or system of Chinese manufacture.

Reasons for this are obvious if we remember that Tea Cultivation and Manufacture in China has scarcely changed over the centuries, and even today, while Tea is cultivated in almost all Chinese provinces, but mainly in the central and southern areas unlike India, Ceylon and other modern Tea Producing Countries, there are no larger estates, and it is still grown along with other crops by peasant proprietors in small patches, from a few bushes to quarter of an acre, on hill slopes. Methods of cultivation and preparation are, therefore, still primitive, and vary widely from one village to the next, and between one district and another.

Robert Fortune brought some Chinese tea makers to India in 1848, and they were sent to Assam and the Kumaon hills to manufacture tea according to their own methods. There were, however, quite a number of Chinamen already in India, as traders, sailors, artisans and coolies, and most of them knew something about the rudiments of tea manufacture as learned in their native land. They soon became aware of the demand for Chinese teamakers in the potential Tea Districts of North-East India, and prospects of a settlement home and good pay encouraged many to offer their services to the planters, and in the 1850's some of them were employed by the early Darjeeling pioneers, by Captain Masson at Tukvar, Mr. Stolke at Steinthal, etc.

The descendants of these Chinese teamakers are still to be found in the Darjeeling District, though none carry on the trade of teamaker. Some married hillwomen and became absorbed into the hill races. The writer knew a most upright and honest old works contractor by the name of Ah Sing, who said his father had come to Darjeeling in the middle 1800's as a teamaker. Ah Sing had married a hillwoman, and during World War II, whenever he was paid for a completed contract, he always insisted upon 10% being deducted from his account for the East India Flight Fund, his contribution to the War Effort. He must have been in his seventies at the time, though he never looked a day over forty. Another of the original Chinese Teamakers became an important Cooly Sirdar at the ill-fated Rhoni Tea Estate. The descendants of others became shoemakers or carpenters, in which trades they have few equals in the world. The descendant of at least one of these early teamakers, married a Bhutia girl and became an Inspector of Police.

N.B. This article is an unedited transcript of a typesript document, undated, in the author's own private collection. As far as is known, it has not been previously published.

Finis.

Appendix 2. *Plate 38*
Map of the Darjeeling District, showing Tea Estates owned or managed by the Wernicke Family.

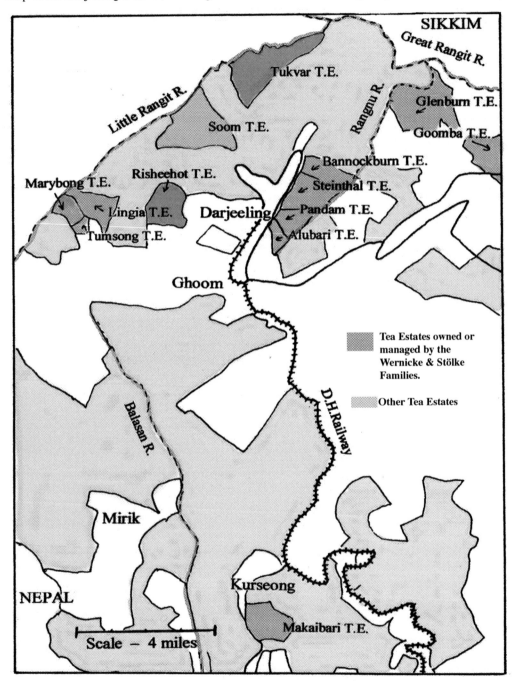

SIKKIM

Great Rangit R.

Tukvar T.E.

Little Rangit R.

Soom T.E.

Rangnu R.

Glenburn T.E.

Goomba T.E.

Bannockburn T.E.

Marybong T.E.

Risheehot T.E.

Steinthal T.E.

Lingia T.E.

Darjeeling

Pandam T.E.

Tumsong T.E.

Alubari T.E.

Ghoom

Tea Estates owned or managed by the Wernicke & Stölke Families.

Other Tea Estates

Balasan R.

D.H.Railway

Mirik

NEPAL

Kurseong

Makaibari T.E.

Scale – 4 miles

Appendix 3. The Wernicke Family Tree.

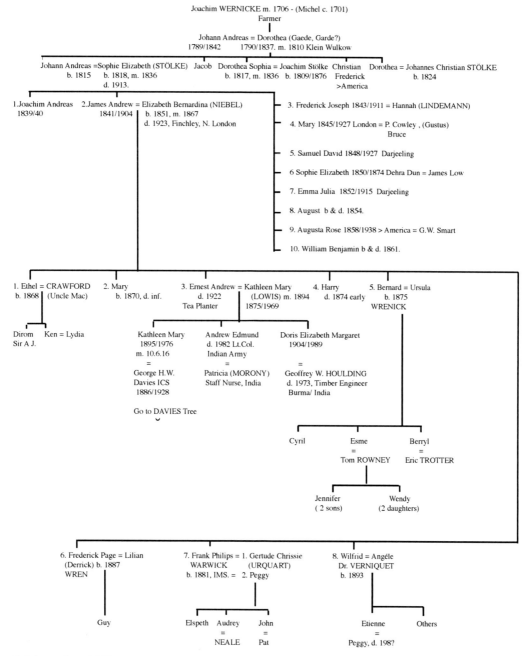

Joachim WERNICKE m. 1706 - (Michel c. 1701)
Farmer

Johann Andreas = Dorothea (Gaede, Garde?)
1789/1842   1790/1837. m. 1810 Klein Wulkow

Johann Andreas =Sophie Elizabeth (STÖLKE)   Jacob   Dorothea Sophia = Joachim Stölke   Christian   Dorothea = Johannes Christian STÖLKE
b. 1815   b. 1818, m. 1836   b. 1817, m. 1836 b. 1809/1876 Frederick   b. 1824
          d. 1913.   >America

1.Joachim Andreas   2.James Andrew = Elizabeth Bernardina (NIEBEL)   3. Frederick Joseph 1843/1911 = Hannah (LINDEMANN)
1839/40   1841/1904   b. 1851, m. 1867
                                 d. 1923, Finchley, N. London   4. Mary 1845/1927 London = P. Cowley , (Gustus)
                                                                                              Bruce

                                                                      5. Samuel David 1848/1927 Darjeeling

                                                                      6 Sophie Elizabeth 1850/1874 Dehra Dun = James Low

                                                                      7. Emma Julia 1852/1915 Darjeeling

                                                                      8. August b & d. 1854.

                                                                      9. Augusta Rose 1858/1938 > America = G.W. Smart

                                                                      10. William Benjamin b & d. 1861.

1. Ethel = CRAWFORD   2. Mary   3. Ernest Andrew = Kathleen Mary   4. Harry   5. Bernard = Ursula
b. 1868   (Uncle Mac) b. 1870, d. inf.   d. 1922   (LOWIS) m. 1894 d. 1874 early   b. 1875
                                    Tea Planter   1875/1969   WRENICK

Dirom   Ken = Lydia   Kathleen Mary   Andrew Edmund   Doris Elizabeth Margaret
Sir A J.   1895/1976   d. 1982 Lt.Col.   1904/1989
                        m. 10.6.16   Indian Army
                        =   =   =
                        George H.W.   Patricia (MORONY)   Geoffrey W. HOULDING
                        Davies ICS   Staff Nurse, India   d. 1973, Timber Engineer
                        1886/1928   Burma/ India

                        Go to DAVIES Tree
                        ◡
                                                                  Cyril   Esme   Berryl
                                                                                =   =
                                                                                Tom ROWNEY   Eric TROTTER

                                                                                Jennifer   Wendy
                                                                                (2 sons)   (2 daughters)

6. Frederick Page = Lilian   7. Frank Philips = 1. Gertude Chrissie   8. Wilfrid = Angéle
(Derrick) b. 1887   WARWICK   (URQUART)   Dr. VERNIQUET
WREN   b. 1881, IMS. = 2. Peggy   b. 1893

        Guy   Elspeth   Audrey   John   Etienne   Others
                                     =   =   =
                                     NEALE   Pat   Peggy, d. 198?

Patriotic name changes in WWI. 3. WERNICKE 5. WRENICK. 6. WREN. 7. WARWICK 8. VERNIQUET.

Appendix 3. The Stölke Family Tree

N.B. Church family registers only restarted after the end of the Thirty Years War.

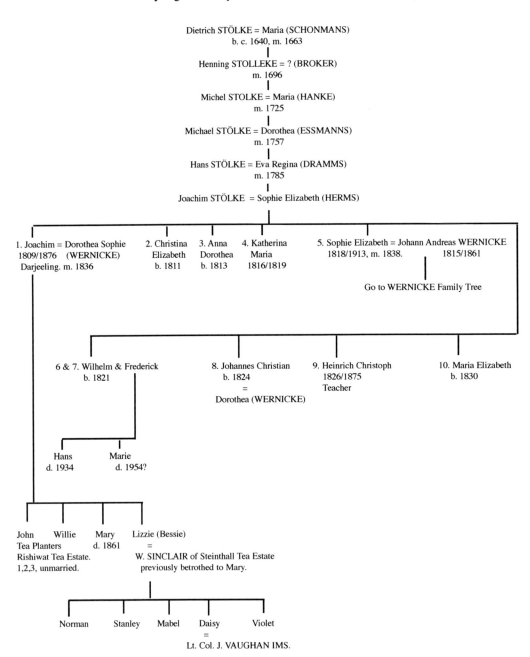

Dietrich STÖLKE = Maria (SCHONMANS)
b. c. 1640, m. 1663

Henning STOLLEKE = ? (BROKER)
m. 1696

Michel STOLKE = Maria (HANKE)
m. 1725

Michael STÖLKE = Dorothea (ESSMANNS)
m. 1757

Hans STÖLKE = Eva Regina (DRAMMS)
m. 1785

Joachim STÖLKE = Sophie Elizabeth (HERMS)

1. Joachim = Dorothea Sophie
1809/1876 (WERNICKE)
Darjeeling. m. 1836

2. Christina
Elizabeth
b. 1811

3. Anna
Dorothea
b. 1813

4. Katherina
Maria
1816/1819

5. Sophie Elizabeth = Johann Andreas WERNICKE
1818/1913, m. 1838.   1815/1861

Go to WERNICKE Family Tree

6 & 7. Wilhelm & Frederick
b. 1821

8. Johannes Christian
b. 1824
=
Dorothea (WERNICKE)

9. Heinrich Christoph
1826/1875
Teacher

10. Maria Elizabeth
b. 1830

Hans
d. 1934

Marie
d. 1954?

John
Tea Planters
Rishiwat Tea Estate.
1,2,3, unmarried.

Willie

Mary
d. 1861

Lizzie (Bessie)
=
W. SINCLAIR of Steinthall Tea Estate
previously betrothed to Mary.

Norman   Stanley   Mabel   Daisy   Violet
=
Lt. Col. J. VAUGHAN IMS.